Smoke Screen

DIANE WINDSOR

Smoke Screen

DIANE WINDSOR

Published and Printed in the United States
by Motina Books.
http://www.MotinaBooks.com

Motina Books
info@motinabooks.com

This is a work of fiction. Names, characters, places, and incidents are the product of the author's imagination or are used fictitiously. Any resemblance to actual persons, living or dead, events, or locales is entirely coincidental.

ISBN-13: 978-1-945060-15-1

DEDICATION

This book is dedicated to my youngest.
I love you more than chocolate.

Saturday Evening

James stuffed the powder that was once a collection of buds, stems, and seeds into the tube he had constructed from PVC piping. He packed it in as tightly as he could.

The sun had begun to set, and the kitchen was not as bright as it had been several minutes ago. The stainless steel refrigerator was casting a shadow along the quartz counter top where all of his supplies were carefully arranged. There was the nine-by-thirteen Pyrex baking dish, coffee filters, a few rubber bands, his mom's Magic Bullet, and a full bottle of butane.

He had already utilized the Magic Bullet to pulverize the leftovers of a really great stash, plus some buds that he had recently dried. That's what was going into the PVC tube, through the open end. The other end was covered by one of the coffee filters and held in place with a rubber band.

Once the tube was full James placed a PVC cap over the open end. This cap had a small hole drilled through the center. It was the same size as the nozzle of the butane canister.

By this time there was barely any sunlight coming into the kitchen window. James switched on the light above the stove, so he could see what he was doing. He realized that in order to have the best visibility, he should just place the Pyrex dish directly on the burners of the gas stove.

He placed the nozzle of the butane can into the hole in the PVC cap, held the end with the coffee filter over the baking dish, and applied steady pressure to the trigger. He didn't have to wait long before a golden liquid started streaming through the coffee filter.

Ah, there it was! Honey oil! James was so excited! He applied the pressure to the canister for about three minutes, until the can was empty and the honey oil ceased flowing. Now he just needed to wait a bit.

He placed the empty canister and the used PVC tube in the sink. He would throw it away later, but he was really hungry now. It was time for some mac and cheese.

About a dozen enamel-covered cast iron skillets and saucepans hung from a rack above his head. James reached for a medium-sized pan, and filled it with water. He set the pan on one of the burners, but before he turned on the gas he made sure to move the Pyrex back to the counter. He wanted to make sure he was being especially cautious.

He turned the stove knob to the "lite" position and listened to the click-click-click of the electronic ignition. That was the last thing he remembered before he heard the deafening roar of the kitchen exploding around him.

Friday—Eight Days Earlier

The strains of *Living On A Prayer* filled the air. The phone sounded much too happy at 5:30 in the morning. She needed to change her alarm; it was ruining her favorite song. Lynda rolled over and slid her finger across the screen. Just five more minutes. Or ten. Fifteen at the most. She rolled out of bed at 5:45 and made her way downstairs. The puppy was at her heels. Well, technically, not a puppy. Fritzi was a five-year-old boxer who was Lynda's shadow. The best dog in the world. She was always up with Lynda, no matter how dark it was outside.

Lynda opened the back door so Fritzi could go outside, then started a pot of coffee. Her morning routine was pretty much the same every weekday. Let the puppy out, clean up any dishes that were left in the sink from dinner the night before, pack her breakfast and lunch, feed the puppy, and make sure that Ben was up in time to catch the school bus.

In the fall of 2013 Ben was just starting the eleventh grade. He was usually pretty good at getting himself up in the morning, showering, and arriving at the bus stop on time. Breakfast consisted of a chocolate-flavored milk drink that supposedly is full of vitamins and minerals.

Lynda was usually able to complete her morning chores

within 45-ish minutes. Then she had time to take a shower, pack her gym bag, and make the bed.

As she fastens the buttons of her blouse, she pokes her head out of the bedroom door, and yells, "Hey, Pumpkin, are you doing okay? Are you almost ready?"

"Yes, Momma, I'm good," came the reply.

"Okay, cool, I'm just about ready to go. Make sure you lock the front door when you leave, honey. I love you!"

"I love you, too!"

Lynda was so lucky; she knew that she could count on Ben doing what he needed to do in order to succeed in school, and help around the house. As a single mom, she needed all the help she could get. If a portion of that help came from her own son, that was even better.

She checked herself in the mirror one last time, before heading out the door. Her dark, shoulder-length hair was smoothly styled for the moment, but she knew it wouldn't last. No matter how hard she tried, her hair frizzed out at least a little bit by lunch time. Sometimes she just put it up, but she didn't think she would today.

There wasn't a dress code at her office so today, like most days, she wore jeans, a button-down shirt, and wedges to work. She didn't know what she would do if she had to wear a suit and pantyhose every day. Probably look for a new job.

She threw her gym and lunch bags in the car, and climbed in after them. Her commute into north Dallas was typically about 40 to 45 minutes, but the audio books she always listened to made that time very close to enjoyable.

Lynda worked as a technical writer for a wireless technology company. Quite often, when she told someone she just met what she did for a living, the response was something like, "That sounds hard!" Sometimes it was, but she enjoyed the work and she was good at it. It was really a matter of translating "engineer language" to "non-engineer language." She worked with engineers and software developers and took the data from their heads, and translated it into a language that non-technical people could understand.

Lynda, Ben, and Lynda's older son, Tim, had moved to Texas from Colorado eight years ago. It was a tough decision; Tim was just getting ready to enter high school, and the little guy was finishing second grade. It was a bad time to uproot the boys, and added to the existing stress of the divorce. Lynda and her husband were splitting up after sixteen years of marriage.

The last thing Lynda wanted to do was cause more chaos for her sons. She was determined to keep the house they had grown up in, and make sure they stayed in school with their friends. She had spent a little over two years at home with them, being a stay-home mom, but now it was time to go back to work. The stay-home mom gig didn't pay very well.

While there were many issues that contributed to the end of Lynda's marriage, the biggest factor was money. Lynda and her ex simply were not on the same page financially. And, to be completely honest, Lynda didn't really have the guts to stand up to him, and insist that they handle their money a little more conservatively.

"Budget" was a four-letter-word in their household. There was no planning, no saving, no working together. If he wanted to buy something, he bought it. That's what credit cards were for, right? He had every new gadget that was on the market. If the letter "I" was at the beginning of a phone's name, he was the first in line. The credit cards were constantly maxed to their limits.

Lynda knew that this wasn't the right way to run a household and raise a family. She just wasn't sure how to fix the problem. The last straw came when her husband was fired from his job for making inappropriate sexual remarks to a coworker. He thought he was being funny, but he wasn't. Instead of hitting the pavement and trying to find a new job, he decided to go into business for himself. This endeavor involved racking up even more debt; he needed a professional website designed, he rented office space. He even hired an organizer and a business advisor! This endeavor of becoming a "telecommunications consultant" was costing much more than Lynda thought it should.

She thought most people started a small business on the kitchen table, starting with one customer, then growing from there. You used what you had – you didn't spend money that wasn't there.

When she tried to broach this point with her husband he just got angry, and told her that she didn't know anything about starting, or running, a business.

"You have to spend money to make money!" was his favorite phrase. He repeated that over and over, up to the point he filed for bankruptcy.

The bills were mounting, the bank accounts were at zero, and the marriage was disintegrating. When Lynda finally told him to leave, he was so entrenched in the "business" that he was happy not to have any other obligations. That's what made it easy to convince him that the best thing for the boys was for the three of them to move to Texas.

Lynda had been applying for many jobs in Colorado, and she had had several interviews; unfortunately, the job offers never followed those interviews. A former coworker of hers had recently moved to Texas, and was trying to convince her to head south.

"There are so many tech jobs down here! You'll never be out of work. And housing is so much more affordable. You can buy a house big enough for all three of you, for less than half the price in Colorado," Renee explained.

Renee was an account executive for a satellite communications company that was headquartered in the Dallas Metroplex. She and Lynda had worked together before Lynda had stopped working to spend some time at home with the kids. Renee had gone through a reduction in force at that job, and had made the move to Texas when she was having a hard time landing a new job in Denver.

"I had three job offers! I actually had to choose the job that was best for me. It was crazy; I ended up interviewing them!"

Renee lived in Plano, Texas, which is a suburb north of Dallas. There are many technology companies around the Plano area, and it's a great place to raise kids, with excellent public schools. It also has a reputation of producing coddled children, thanks to their helicopter parents, but Renee didn't share that. She knew that Lynda wasn't that kind of mom.

Lynda was beginning to consider making the move, but she still didn't want to uproot the boys. But, the more interviews she went on without getting an offer, the more she was beginning to consider other options.

She perused the job sites several times a day, and received all the alerts for "technical writer" and "south

Denver." On a whim, she decided to add a new location to her search parameters – "Plano, Texas." There were too many results to be displayed on the screen; Lynda needed to click the **Next Page** link twice in order to see them all.

This was three times the number of available tech writer jobs in Denver! She perused the job listings, not really thinking she would actually apply for any. But then she saw one that looked like it was made for her. She had worked in that exact field of wireless telecommunications for several years, and written numerous documents. It couldn't hurt to send a resume and see what happens.

An hour later, while she was driving to the elementary school to pick up her youngest from school, her cell phone rang. The area code displayed on the phone was "972."

She hesitated before answering. What if this job in Texas worked out? Was she really ready for this kind of change? She clicked the answer button.

"Hello, this is Lynda."

"Hi Lynda, this is Cathy with Wireless Telex in Plano. I'd like to set up a telephone interview between you and our engineering manager. What's a good time for you?"

From that point forward, everything just happened in a blur. Lynda had never gone through a job interviewing and hiring process so quickly in her life. Applying for a hostess job at Bennigan's when she was in college took longer than getting this job offer. They didn't even want to meet her in person before the engineer manager made the verbal offer. The next day, the written offer arrived at her house via Fed Ex. They were serious.

Wireless Telex didn't even have a problem with the fact that she wasn't local. They were offering a little help with relocation expenses, which Lynda really appreciated.

Lynda went through this process without including her ex. She felt that since he was making important decisions without her input (like not getting a job and contributing to the family financially), she could pursue a different path without consulting him. Especially since this job she was considering would be beneficial to the family, and not propel them into bankruptcy.

She was nervous about talking to him about the job and, even more than the job, the move. She had spoken to the boys, and while they weren't thrilled with the decision, they understood. Lynda did her best to explain the practical aspects, like being able to find a job and afford a house with only one household income. She also explained that their dad was welcome to come with them. She just didn't think he'd want to.

Lynda was right. She suspected he was pleased that he wouldn't have any responsibilities. He would be completely free to focus on the business, and on himself. And Lynda would be free to rebuild her career, her bank account, and her family.

Lynda began the painstaking process of getting the house ready to put on the market. Over the following two weeks the house was filled with painters, carpet cleaners, window washers, and a guy who refinished the wood floors. When the house was finally listed, it didn't take long for it to sell.

Wireless Telex was great about letting her work from Colorado until she was ready to move to Texas. She flew to Texas once to meet the team and learn what her responsibilities would be. Until she closed on the house in Denver, she could just hang out there, and write about AT commands and how to configure wireless modems.

It was a good thing that she was only gone for five days. During that time, her ex forgot about their youngest son's birthday, and the dog was left alone for too long, which resulted in pee all over the upstairs carpet. The carpet that no longer belonged to them, because the house had already been sold. She grabbed the carpet shampooer, filled it with hot water, and did her best to get the stain out.

Lynda spent the time before the closing cleaning out the basement and having garage sales. She wanted to take as few items as possible to Texas to make a really fresh start. They had too much crap, anyway. Most people did, didn't they? She and the boys packed the household items, clothing, and toys.

Springtime in Colorado can be a little crazy. While they were taking a pizza break from packing boxes one grey Saturday afternoon, it started to snow. Without a word, Tim left the table. He went out to the garage, grabbed his bike, and rode through the swirling flurries.

Lynda stood up from the table and moved to the window to watch him ride around the cul-de-sac. Snow was sprinkled in his dark hair. He rode around and around, popping an occasional wheelie. After about ten minutes he rode his bike up the driveway, dropped it in the garage, and came through the door.

His cheeks were pink; snowflakes covered his hair and his long eyelashes. Why do boys so often have such thick, gorgeous eyelashes?

Tim placed his freezing hands on his mom's cheeks. Lynda shrieked! He replied with laughter.

"I just wanted to see if I would really miss the snow, but I think I'll be okay."

Escrow closed without a hitch.

Renee helped find a rental in a good North Texas neighborhood, with good schools. They settled in Rosemeade, Texas; a suburb north of Dallas.

Lynda packed up the boys, left her ex in charge of himself and his business, and headed south.

Lynda was at her desk with a cup of coffee by 8:15. She was working on a new user manual that explained how to use a new vehicle tracker. The target market for this tracker was parents who want to make sure their newly-licensed teenagers weren't breaking any traffic laws. Messages were sent from the tracker to a web app that indicated exactly where the car was, and how fast it was going.

Lynda thought this was a great way to have a little extra control over teenagers who thought they were better drivers than their parents. Which, coincidentally, were all of them.

The meeting reminder on her computer beeped; she grabbed her coffee, phone, notebook and a pen, and headed to her 9:00. As she was making mental notes about the engineering meeting, she also thought about what Ben was doing. School started at 8:30, so he was in first period right now. Art. She knew that he had a sketching project due the following week.

That's one big difference between moms and dad. When dads were at work, they were completely focused on the task at hand. They did a great job at what they were doing, but they couldn't think about anything else. Moms, on the other hand, did what they needed to do, but what their kids were doing were always in the back of their minds. Always.

Lynda knew when Ben was on the bus going to school, when he was at school, when he was on the bus on the way home, and when he was home. He always checked in with his mom when he went to hang out with his friends. And his friends are great! Even though Ben isn't into sports, he hangs out with kids who are on the football and wrestling teams. They're the good kids. She had nothing to worry about.

Lynda met Scott in the conference room. He was your typical Electrical Engineer; he wore jeans and a t-shirt to work, and those weird toe-shoes. Sure, so it was a Friday, which meant that the usual casual attire was now ultra-casual. But toe-shoes? Really? Scott wore his long hair in a ponytail. Okay, maybe he didn't look like most Double-Es. But he knew his stuff, and took the time that Lynda needed until she completely understood the how a product worked, and what the target audience needed to understand about it.

Lynda got along with all of the guys. Engineers hate writing manuals, so they were more than happy to spend a relatively small amount of time with Lynda, if it meant that they didn't have to do the actual writing. After about an hour and a half of hearing about satellite communication and the 900MHz frequency, Lynda felt she had enough information to start the user guide.

The rest of the day passed uneventfully. She went to the nearby gym on her lunch hour and ran a few miles; one of the wonderful perks of her job! Employers know that employees who exercise regularly take fewer sick days, so they all reap the benefits.

Ben was already home when Lynda arrived. She could hear him plucking the strings of his bass. He and some buddies had started a band, but they hadn't booked any gigs yet. They sure practiced a lot, so they must be getting ready to put on a great show.

"Hey, sweetie, do you have any homework this weekend?" she called up the stairs.

"No, Momma, but I'm gonna go hang out with my friends tonight."

"Okay, no prob!"

That meant that her butt had a hot date with the couch and the remote control was all hers. She settled in for the evening with a bowl of popcorn, and *The Notebook*. Fritzi curled up on the couch beside her.

The movie credits started rolling when she decided to check in with Ben; it was 10:00 and he wasn't home yet. Not a big deal – the curfew for teens was midnight, but she still needed to know where he was.

Lynda: Are you coming home soon?

Ben: Can I sleep over at Michael's house? His mom said it's okay.

Lynda: Sure, honey, that's fine.

Ben: Okay, thanks Momma. Love you.

Lynda: Love you too, sweetie.

Lynda clicked off the TV and headed up to bed. Fritzi was right behind her.

Very Early Saturday Morning

"Dude, hand over that doobie. You're hogging it!"

Ben chuckled. "'Doobie?' Man, how old are you? I think that word disappeared with the seventies."

He handed another boy the little bit that remained. He watched his friend inhale deeply; the tip glowed brightly in the dark suburban night.

"Okay, you've had enough!" Ben snatched the joint back, and jogged a few feet ahead of his friend. He didn't feel like sharing anymore.

The three boys were about the same age. They would all celebrate their seventeenth birthdays the following spring. Ben was a little shorter than the others; five feet, nine inches, compared to his friends' height of almost six feet. His hair was thick and dark, like his mom's, and almost touched his shoulders these days. Also like his mom's. His sparkling blue eyes were framed by thick, black hipster-type glasses.

It was 3:00am; well past the city curfew for sixteen-year-olds. The boys were roaming the suburban streets, stopping every now and then to roll a new joint. There was no destination at the end of this journey; they simply chose one of the many quiet, suburban neighborhoods and wandered for hours as they smoked.

This was quickly becoming a weekend tradition. Sometimes one of the boys brought booze, sometimes even some painkillers that someone swiped from their parents' medicine cabinet, but most of the time it was pot. It was easy to get weed in the suburbs. Several of Ben's classmates always seemed to have plenty available. He wasn't sure how they acquired it. He didn't really care, as long as they had some for him.

"Ben, what did you tell your mom tonight?" asked Joe.

"That I'm staying over at Michael's tonight," Ben replied. "She never checks up on me."

"Ha ha! That's awesome."

"I know, right!" replied Ben. "She trusts me completely." That struck him as very funny, and he doubled over in laughter.

Ben loved being out in the middle of the night. It was the only time he truly felt happy, and at peace with the world.

The rest of the time, Ben and his friends were annoyed. They were annoyed with school and annoyed with their parents. Ben felt that it was time for him to live on his own and be independent, but unfortunately society didn't agree with him. He already knew so much about the world, more than most adults, he was certain. His mom thought she did, but she didn't. How could she? She just went to work and came home. She never experienced anything. Well, she ran races and did volunteer work, but that isn't what life is about.

Life is about pushing limits and living on the edge! Ben wanted to dance all night long and surf the crowd at a killer rock concert. He wanted to jump out of an airplane. He wanted tattoos. And he didn't think he needed to have anyone's permission for anything.

As far as he was concerned, teachers, parents and the police were all ultra-conservative assholes who were completely out of touch with reality. What did it matter if he listened to music during class, if he already understood the lesson, and really didn't need to pay attention? It didn't! But the damn teacher sent him to the principal's office anyway.

It was the same with cops, but at a slightly different level. There were so many ridiculous rules to follow. There is absolutely nothing wrong with marijuana. It should absolutely be legal, without exception. People who are stoned are never angry—you never hear about a man beating the crap out of his wife because he was smoking some pot. And you never see a "mean stoner," like you do a "mean drunk." Alcohol is much more dangerous than pot, but it's legal. That made no sense to Ben.

Ben took a drag on the joint. He inhaled very deeply, and held it in as long as he could. Oh, yeah, that's the stuff.

He loved being out in the middle of the night. The streets were quiet and relatively cool, even in the Texas summers. Well, cool by Texas standards, anyway. On the dark, suburban streets, with his friends and his weed, he could relax. He could breathe. He didn't have to deal with teachers or his mom.

Just as the last bit of smoke left his lips, a bright light shone directly in his eyes. He was blinded.

"Gentlemen, you're out kind of late tonight, aren't you?" said a booming voice.

The boys were silent. They didn't know what to say.

"What are your names?" asked the officer.

"Uh, isn't like 10:00?" asked Ben.

"No, it's 2:00 in the morning," replied the officer. "What are you boys doing out here?"

"We're just going for a walk, sir," said Ben. "We're on our way home right now."

"I'll need your parents' phone numbers to make sure."

Oh, crap.

There it was again; *Living On A Prayer*. Lynda was awakened from a very sound sleep. She really needed to change her ringtone. Her favorite song was being ruined. What time was it, anyway? She looked at the clock displayed on her phone; it told her it was 3:17am.

She was instantly terrified. Nothing good ever came from a phone call in the middle of the night.

The display on her phone showed her older son's name. Oh, Lord, what was wrong with Tim?

"Tim? What's wrong?" she asked breathlessly.

"I'm okay Mom. I'm here with Ben."

"You're at Michael's house?" she asked. Ben had told her he was sleeping at Michael's. Where else could he possibly be?

"No, we're over by the middle school. He and two friends were picked up by the police. They were walking around after curfew."

"What?" she must still be fuzzy from sleep. He couldn't have just said what she thought he said.

"They want to know if it's okay with you that I bring him home. Here's the officer."

A new voice came on the phone.

"Hi Mrs. Murphy, this is Officer Schaefer. I came upon your son and his friends walking around, and they're not supposed to be out this late. Is it all right with you if your other son brings him home?"

"Yes, of course, that's fine! Thank you so much, Officer."

Lynda and Fritzi sat on the bottom of the stairs, both of them fixated on the front door. Fritzi wasn't quite sure what was so interesting about that door, but if Lynda was interested, then so was she.

Lynda was absently scratching the top of the dog's head. It's amazing how comforting a pup can be when you're nervous, sad or scared. Maybe it's because dogs always love you, no matter what. They have a kind of sixth sense.

How long does it take a couple of boys to drive a few blocks? They should have been home by now. She stared at the front door, willing it to open.

What the hell was going on with Ben? He had never done this kind of thing before; blatant disobedience. At least, she didn't think he had. Sure, sometimes he misbehaved at school, but he's a boy. Lynda occasionally received phone calls or e-mails from teachers, but the offenses were never that serious. He's an active, curious boy who doesn't like to sit still for very long. But it wasn't a big deal. At least, she didn't think it was.

Finally, she saw headlights shining through the window. Lynda opened the door as her two sons came up the walkway.

"What were you doing out there?" she asked Ben.

They stood in the foyer, not saying a word. Ben had an odd look on his face; kind of a smile, but not really a smile. Tim and Lynda were staring at him. His face looked so strange, but Lynda couldn't put her finger on the problem.

She had to look up in order to really see his eyes. At five

feet, eight inches, Ben practically towered over his mother. Linda was only five feet, three inches, so it wasn't hard for her kids to be taller than she was.

But his eyes…they looked swollen. His bottom lids were so puffy, it looked like he was almost squinting.

"Are you high?" she asked him.

"No," he replied. "Can I go to bed?"

There was no reason to keep him up. They could talk more in the morning.

"Yes, go ahead," she told him.

Ben quickly disappeared upstairs. Once he was out of sight, Tim turned to her.

"Mom," he said, "Don't believe for a minute that he isn't stoned."

"Oh, I don't think so," Lynda replied. "He doesn't do that kind of thing."

"How do you know?"

"I just asked him, and he said he wasn't high."

"Mom, you're being really naïve," said Tim. "Why else would he sneak out in the middle of the night? You saw his eyes, didn't you? He's baked!"

Lynda didn't know what to say. She stood there staring at her eldest in disbelief.

"You go home," she told her son. "We both need some sleep. I'll think about what to do tomorrow. Thanks for bringing him home."

Tim could see how distressed his mother was. He wrapped his arms around her and said, "It's okay, Mom. I love you."

She followed him out the front door.

"Tim," she called. "Did you do this kind of crap when

you were sixteen and I just didn't know about it?"

He chuckled. "No, Mom, that wasn't really my thing when I was in high school. Get some sleep."

"Get some sleep." That was easy for Tim to say! Lynda went back to bed, but she couldn't get her mind to turn off.

What had gotten into her youngest son? For so many years, they had been so close. Lynda had always been very involved in his extra-curricular activities. She had attended so many third-grade basketball practices and games; she was even the statistics mom!

At each game she kept track of the how many baskets each boy made, how many assists and how many rebounds. She loved being involved with his activities; she was all he had, so she had to. And she was proud of it! Even though his dad wasn't in the picture, he did not miss out on the things little boys wanted to do.

When Ben was in Cub Scouts, she could make a Pinewood Derby car with the best of them. Ben had even won trophies for the cars they made together!

So when did he start pulling stunts like this? Sneaking out in the middle of the night and getting high; when did this start?

Ben had always been affectionate with her. They gave each other big hugs every day, and said, "I love you" all the time. Even when they were just sending text messages, they finished with, "I love you."

Lynda and her son had a positive, strong relationship. She was sure of it. She finally started to fall asleep just as the sun was rising.

Lynda dragged herself out of bed around eleven, still

feeling very groggy. She didn't function well when her sleep was interrupted by a teenager who got busted for sneaking out in the middle of the night. She splashed water on her face and smoothed down her dark hair, which was sticking up in a million different directions. If anyone ever sponsored a bed-head contest, she'd take first place for sure.

Sunlight streamed through the bathroom window; Texas fall weather was fantastic. It was that perfect blend between the wet, chilly winter, and the roasting, suffocating heat of summer. Fall was when Lynda could open all the windows in the house, and let the breeze freshen the stale, inside air.

It was also great running weather. She would schedule four miles today. Lynda often scheduled her day around her running plans. Priorities, right?

She and Fritzi shuffled into the kitchen to start a pot of coffee. Lynda was just pouring her first cup when Ben came charging into the kitchen.

"Hi Momma," he said. His skateboard was tucked under his arm. "I'm going to go hang out with some friends."

"No you're not!" Lynda replied, incredulously. What was he thinking? After being caught in the middle of the night by the police, he thought he could come and go as he pleased? No sir! She was going to talk, and he was going to listen.

Her hand gripped the coffee mug tightly. Anger was rising inside of her like steam in a kettle, ready to boil. "You're grounded. You're not going anywhere."

Her baby boy looked at her, and smiled. Actually, it was more like an evil grin than a friendly smile.

"I'll be around later, but now I'm going out with my

friends. See ya."

And that was it; he walked out, while his mother stood staring at the door that closed behind him.

The anger she felt was still there, but it was joined by fear. This situation was quickly spinning out of control. She was losing the respect that she deserved as a mother. She didn't know who this kid was anymore; where had her son gone?

There was a bedroom upstairs that was once occupied by an adorable little boy. His big, blue eyes sparkled, and his bright smile was usually missing a tooth here and there.

Overnight this sweet little guy had disappeared, and in his place stood a hulking, towering man-child. Okay, maybe five-feet-eight wasn't really "towering," but it wasn't hard to tower over Lynda's five-foot-three-inch frame. Those blue eyes of his were now often dark with frustration and anger, and that scared her.

Could she physically restrain him if she needed to? No, of course not. Would he actually try to hurt her? She couldn't imagine that he would. But, she hadn't imagined that her little angel would sneak out of the house in the middle of the night, either.

What the hell was she in for?

Lynda's parenting philosophy had always been to trust her kids unless they gave her a reason not to. She had always believed that she knew what her kids were doing because she was so involved with their lives. As a single mom, she made an extra effort to know the teachers, coaches, and also their friends' parents.

But the behavior that Ben was displaying was a pretty good reason to start questioning that trust.

She stood at the foot of the stairs, staring toward the

second floor and contemplating what she was about to do. She had to discover the extent of Ben's transgressions. Many parents she knew believed in letting their children have complete privacy. Their bedroom was their own personal domain, and parents had no right to enter without the children's permission. Lynda didn't completely agree with that. That bedroom was still in her house, wasn't it? She's the one who makes the mortgage payment, puts food on the table, and clothes on her son's back. Exactly what rights does he think he has?

Of course, it's important to treat children with love, kindness, and respect. But respect isn't automatic; it has to be earned, like trust has to be earned. As far as Lynda was concerned, trust and respect for Ben were out the window. She had every right to go through his room and see what she could find.

She climbed the stairs, armed only with her hot coffee.

Ben's room was probably just like any other sixteen-year-old boy's but it still drove Lynda crazy. The floor was littered with jeans, t-shirts and underwear. She couldn't see the surface of his desk, because of empty soda cans, and paper that looked like it should be in the trash. The blinds were closed tightly, and the faint odor of boy-feet lingered in the air.

The only time this room was really clean was when Lynda tackled it herself. That project occurred about once a year, when Ben was out of the house for a couple of days. She tried to routinely go through the closet to donate clothing that no longer fit Ben. She made sure that toys were put away, and that trash was thrown away. Well, at sixteen there weren't as many toys as there used to be. She supposed the Xbox games counted as toys, and they were all over the place. The games were on one side of the room, and the cases on another.

There were four skateboards in the room, in addition to the one he had left the house with. Skateboarding was, of course, his main form of transportation.

Lynda contemplated her plan of attack. Typical hiding places that a teenager would consider include the dresser drawers, under the mattress and the closet. But what about the atypical hiding places? Lynda tried to switch her brain into teenager mode. Where would he hide something he really didn't want anyone to find? Were there boxes with false bottoms? Coke cans that were converted to storage containers for weed?

She would certainly check the obvious places. It's possible that he thought he was in the clear, and that she wouldn't go through his room. She never had before. Up to now she had truly trusted him, and granted the privacy he thought he deserved.

She set her coffee cup on top of the dresser and opened the top drawer. As expected, it was full of underwear and socks, stuffed almost to overflowing. Lynda dug through all of the pieces of clothing, squeezing each piece in case something was hidden between the folds and wrinkles. Her hands moved to the back of the drawer, searching the corners and the edges. Nothing.

She repeated this process inside the other two drawers, with the same result. Not a gosh-darn thing.

But that was okay. The dresser was the most obvious hiding place. She didn't expect to find anything too interesting there.

It occurred to her that under the dresser might be a good hiding place. A small LED flashlight sat on Ben's desk. Lynda picked it up and clicked the button on the bottom to turn it on. She knelt in front of the dresser, and aimed the light into the gloom.

She saw plenty of dust bunnies, and a couple of candy wrappers. Yuck. An empty can of Dr. Pepper was also rolling around down there. It occurred to her that the underside of the dresser would be a fabulous hiding place. Had it occurred to Ben?

Her fingers slid along the smooth wood, feeling for anything that shouldn't be there. It would be so easy to grab some duct tape and plaster a contraband item to the bottom of the dresser. She searched diligently, but didn't come up with anything.

"Okay," she said out loud. "Not a problem. There's a lot of room left." Lynda sipped her coffee and checked out the room, considering the next potential hiding place.

Next stop, under the mattress. Ben had a queen-sized bed, so there was a lot of real estate to cover. First, she thought she'd take a peek under the bed. She flipped on the little flashlight again and was face-to-face with a Tyrannosaurus-Rex hand puppet. A wave of nostalgia came over her. This puppet had belonged to Tim when he was about five! Oh, goodness, her boys had once been so little. Now, she had to stand on tip-toe to even get close to looking each one in the eye. Geez, where does the time go?

She pulled out the puppet and shined the light through the gloom. There was a collection of Nerf dart guns and some stray socks, but nothing that looked particularly incriminating. Just like with the dresser, she did her best to check the underside of the box spring, to see if anything had been taped there. There was nothing.

Lynda stood up and stretched; now, she supposed she

should check under the mattress. That wasn't going to be easy. Mattresses are heavy! She remembered when she and the boys had moved into their house, almost eight years ago. The three of them had had a heck of a time lugging three heavy mattresses up the stairs, and into the bedrooms. Half-way up the staircase there was a sharp right turn, which made moving furniture nearly impossible.

She concluded that the best way to tackle the mattress was a little bit at a time. She should be able to lift each corner and get a good view of what was underneath. Bending her knees, she grabbed one corner and lifted it as high as she could. She was actually able to lift it higher than she had thought she could. This gave her a good view of about half the space between the mattress and the box spring. And what a view it was!

Lynda had unearthed a teenage boy's mother lode. She felt like Indiana Jones, conquering a multitude of dangerous obstacles, in order to discover the Holy Grail. Spread out in front of her where several Playboys, what looked like packages of rolling papers, and one other item that was very interesting; an iPod. The reason it was so interesting, was that Lynda didn't recognize it. She had bought all of Ben's electronic gadgets, so she knew what they looked like. She had never seen this one. It was an older model, and the screen was cracked.

She pressed the power button, and the screen glowed. No pass code was required; she had gotten lucky! She didn't think her adorable teen would be too willing to provide her with that, if it had been needed.

Lynda slipped the iPod in the pocket of her jeans for the time being. She wanted to finish searching the bedroom, before taking the time to investigate what was on that iPod. She wasn't planning on giving it back to Ben any time soon. The Playboys and papers remained where they were. Her goal was to make sure that the room didn't look like she had torn it apart looking for incriminating evidence.

The issue about whether or not a teenager deserves their privacy is very controversial. Lynda used to work with a gentleman who told her that as soon as his son turned eighteen, he stopped keeping tabs on him. This boy basically had the run of the house. In her friend's mind, just because this kid had circled the sun eighteen times, he was now a responsible adult. He wasn't even expected to pay rent in exchange for the privilege of privacy and un-earned respect. This young man had all of the privilege of being an adult, with none of the responsibility.

Lynda didn't agree with that philosophy. If a child, no matter how old, was living under her roof, then he needed to follow the rules of her household. That included obeying curfews, no drug and alcohol use, and pulling his weight with chores.

In her heart, she really wanted to trust her son. She wanted to believe everything he told her; that he was doing his homework, and hanging out with the good kids. But now, all that trust was gone; it had disappeared. It takes years to build trust. It can be lost in an instant.

She returned to her task. In addition to the dresser and the bed, the closet was the next best place to look. Lynda opened the door, and gasped in surprise. "Oh my God," she said aloud. It was a total disaster area. Lynda thought it looked like a bomb had gone off, and left a pile of teenage boy crap. Empty hangers hung on the rod. The clothes that were supposed to be on them were piled in a huge mound on the floor. In addition to the jeans, shirts, pajama bottoms and shoes, the mound consisted of books, papers, and empty soda cans. At least, that was what she could see. Who knew what lurked in the middle of the pile. Lynda really didn't want to find out.

There were several built-in shelves on the side of the closet. They weren't quite as disgusting as the pile on the floor. She investigated the shelves, but didn't really see anything too suspicious. There were some shoes that Ben didn't wear often, and some old toys, from when he was a little guy. Ben used to love Legos. He would spend hours following the instructions, searching for the right piece, and putting together all kinds of spaceships and cities.

He especially loved the Star Wars sets. When he was ten he spent about six weeks putting together the Death Star. Lynda had spent hours with him, helping him search for the pieces he needed. Geez, there were so many! There were over 3,400 pieces in that set, and it was designed for kids who were at least sixteen years old. But, here was little Ben, who was dying to have it for this tenth birthday.

As he built it, they discovered that it was a bit lopsided and heavier on one side. It crashed twice during the building process. The first time it happened there were tears, and the second time, he said he was done with it. Lynda didn't push him. She knew he'd get back to it when he was ready. She was the one who came up with the idea to build a base for it, and superglue some of the bricks together so it would be more sturdy. That actually worked, and the Death Star held a place of honor right in the entryway of their home for a long time. That way, everyone who entered would see it and hear the story of how Ben had built it.

But now, it was resigned to live in the dark closet with the nasty pile of boy things. Just looking at it brought Lynda back to earlier, happier times, when her little boy was still her little boy. She knew that all children grew up, and that it's her job as a parent to raise him to successful adulthood. She just wasn't feeling very successful at that moment, and she longed for the times when he was still her little pumpkin. Maybe they should sell the Death Star, so another little boy could enjoy it. That might be a good idea.

Lynda forced herself to return to the present, and looked at the pile again. She really, really didn't want to start rummaging through it. But she probably had to. There might be something really interesting buried within its murky depths. Yuck.

She decided that she needed to go through it, item by item, and see what surfaced. Each grubby shoe and nasty t-shirt that she pulled from the closet lay temporarily on the floor in the bedroom. The plan was to put the pile back in the closet when she was finished.

Geez, there were so many dirty clothes! She knew that Ben had a clothes hamper in here somewhere. She bought a new one just a few months ago. The flimsy nylon hampers don't last very long. The wires had been poking out of it and there were holes in the nylon sides. Lynda had purchased a sturdy wicker one to replace it. Why couldn't Ben just put his laundry where it belonged? She knew the answer; because he was a teen-aged boy.

She continued rummaging through the pile, and she really didn't think she would find anything either interesting or incriminating. However, beneath a wrinkled and stained Grouplove t-shirt, Lynda discovered an item that didn't seem to belong. A long, clear, flexible tube that was connected to a funnel. She picked it up, and looked at it curiously.

"What the heck is this?" she said aloud. She examined the tubing and the funnel, and couldn't imagine what it was for. Then she sniffed it, and was struck by the realization. Her college life in the dorms of Colorado State University came rushing back.

A beer bong had been stashed in the pile of Ben's dirty laundry. Great. And, it had obviously been used at some point since it reeked of beer.

"One more item to confiscate," she thought.

Lynda spent a little more time digging through the pile, and she quickly examined the rest of the closet, but she felt fairly confident that she had uncovered everything there was to find. Her goal had been to gather information. She didn't want Ben to become overly suspicious, and possibly start hiding his loot somewhere outside of the house. Her decision to leave the rolling papers under the mattress was based on the fact that that particular hiding place seemed to Lynda like the main hiding place. That's where the most important, and the most current, treasure was buried.

She had the notion that the pile in the closet was meant to conceal items for the long term. The beer bong had been buried under items of clothing and shoes that Lynda hadn't seen her son wear in months. The Grouplove concert where Ben had purchased the shirt had taken place the previous year. He had worn the shirt almost daily right after the concert, but hardly at all since then. So, Lynda was pretty darn sure that he did not stash things in the closet regularly. The beer bong was from a while ago. If she took it, she doubted that it would be missed.

She brought her spoils into her own bedroom, and punched in the combination of her small safe. The safe was mainly used for the cash she kept on hand, and important papers such as her passport and their birth certificates. But she wasn't willing to take the chance that one day while she was at work, Ben would decide to start rummaging through her own closet and dresser.

There was plenty of room for the iPod and the beer bong. Once they were safely locked away, Lynda returned to her son's room. She returned it to a state similar to the one she had found it in, and turned the light off. She was done for now.

The process of tossing her youngest son's bedroom in search of drugs and drug paraphernalia had left Lynda feeling extremely stressed. She knew that she needed to do something with this new information, but she wasn't sure what. Should she go to the police? To the school? Could his father help? Ugh, she needed to clear her head!

Lynda knew that the best way to clear her head and reduce a bit of the stress she was feeling was to go for a run. She was an avid runner; she made a point to run at least four days each week, for about four miles each time. It was her thing. It was what kept her both physically and mentally healthy.

She often ran with music, but felt that during this run, she needed to think and keep her mind free of any external interference. The morning was bright and warm, but the Texas heat wasn't as intense as it had been just a few short months before.

Her GPS watch beeped at her and said, "Activity started." So, she started.

Lynda liked to think of herself as a problem solver. If

she didn't know how to fix something, she could learn how. She thought of the time that she needed to replace an electrical outlet in her home. Just because she had never done such a thing before, didn't mean she couldn't. That's what YouTube was for, right? Teaching single moms how to fix things around the house. She certainly couldn't afford to shell out cash to electricians, plumbers, and painters every time she needed to have something done around the house.

The rhythm of her feet hitting the ground almost matched the rhythm of her breathing. One mile was already in the books, and her head was feeling lighter. It always happened that way. Lynda could be weighed down by the worst problem she could possibly imagine; and then she goes for a run. She always wondered how the process of physically exerting herself caused her to feel better both mentally and emotionally. She wondered, but didn't question it too hard. She just enjoyed it.

As she ran she considered her plan. She would attack this problem the same way she attacked any other problem; she'd start with the Internet. That's where everyone started, when they needed to learn something new.

Lynda also started thinking about any other kids who might be doing drugs with Ben. That word struck her. Drugs? Did she think he was involved in something more serious than marijuana? Sure, that was serious enough in its own right. Several states across the nation were beginning to legalize the use of recreational marijuana, but Texas was not one of them. And, she knew that even if they lived in a state where using cannabis was legal, it was still absolutely illegal for minors to partake.

But what if it becomes, or had already become, more than that? It was still controversial as to whether the use of marijuana could act as a gateway to the use of more dangerous drugs.

She would need to research all of that.

Lynda felt that the Internet probably wouldn't be enough. There must be people in the community, other parents, teachers, counselors, and law enforcement, who could educate her and help her. Lynda wasn't shy, and she had no problem reaching out to others for information.

Speaking of "reaching out," should she contact the parents of the kids Ben was spending time with? She wasn't sure who they were, but she could probably find out. Even if her son didn't want to tell her, she would find out. Lynda could always start with the parents of kids she'd known for years. She would find someone who'd be willing to talk to her. Kids love to talk.

After two more miles, Lynda started feeling like she wasn't as completely out of control as she had first thought. The clarity was addicting! Who needed drugs when you could go for a run?

Lynda ran a total of four miles that day. She walked the last few blocks back to the house, thinking about her plan. She felt that the iPod she had discovered would probably hold a lot of information. Why else would it be tucked between the mattress and box spring?

She would start with that.

Saturday Afternoon

Ben wasn't home yet when Lynda walked inside, but that didn't surprise her. It was getting more and more difficult for her to get him to stick around. She understood that; teenagers have a need to feel independent and test their limits. That was fine, as long as those limits weren't illegal or dangerous.

Teenagers need to stretch their wings and learn how to be independent. This is how they learn to be self-sufficient adults. People often talk about "raising children," but in Lynda's opinion, she was raising an adult. Who wants to have a 25-year-old child living in their room, playing video games all day? It's Lynda's responsibility as a parent to raise an adult who will be a contributing member of society. This was a difficult task to accomplish on her own.

She longed to have a strong, positive male role model for her son. A couple years ago, she had contacted Big Brothers and put Ben on the list so he could have a strong male role model in his life. But she was told at that time that there was a shortage of men in the program. "We have plenty of women in the Big Sisters program," said the lady on the phone. Ben didn't need a big sister; Lynda was already involved in his school life and extra-curricular activities. What he needed was a man to teach him how to become a man.

Lynda didn't like to play the single mom card. She never told people her story when she first met them because she didn't want anyone to feel sorry for her. She didn't think of herself as a victim, or as someone who needed a handout. Her job was to do whatever it took to raise her children, and build a good life for her family. She did her best by having a good job, knowing her son's friends and their parents, and spending time with him. But she knew it wasn't enough. In an ideal situation, Ben's father would have been there to help raise their son. This wasn't an ideal situation.

She walked into the bathroom, turned on the shower and waited for the water to get steamy. While she waited, she thought it might be a good time to take a look at the iPod. She punched in the combination of the safe, and grabbed it from its hiding place. It was an iPod Touch, so it looked just like an iPhone, but it didn't have the cellular functionality. Lynda knew that with a WiFi connection, it could do pretty much everything that an iPhone could do.

The iPod contained the all the standard apps; browser, messaging, camera, and, of course, the music player. Lynda started with the messaging app. There were a couple messages, but nothing incriminating. Questions about school assignments, and meeting for a burger. Huh – that was surprising. She had been certain that in the messages app, she would find something that would tell her more about Ben's recent activity.

She used her index finger to swipe to the next screen. That's where she noticed the little white bird silhouette against the blue background. The Twitter app is installed on this iPod. It might not mean anything, but it was certainly worth looking into. She tapped the icon to launch the app.

She wasn't prompted for login credentials; they were apparently saved by the app. As she expected, Lynda saw her son's main Twitter page, with tweets from him and his friends. At the bottom of the screen was a small envelope icon, with the label, "Messages." She tapped the envelope lightly. Before her, in blue and white message bubbles, were many messages between Ben and someone with the Twitter handle, "SupaFreek."

Ben: Can you bring some stuff to school tomorrow?

SupaFreek: Yeah, man. I got some og kush. Meet before school?

Ben: Yeah, at the usual spot.

"Oh my God," Lynda said out loud. "They're bringing it to school?"

There were also messages from someone called, "Legalize." Those were recent, within the last few hours.

Legalize: We're meeting at the bluffs. Bring snacks.

Ben: I'll be there soon!

"Bring snacks?" What did that mean?

Lynda continued scrolling through the Twitter messages. There were several names she saw over and over. "Maryjane," and "Ztoner," appeared everywhere. In all of these messages there were references to dabs, papers, popcorn, dro and shwag. What were they talking about?

There were also messages about, "Let's go fly kites later today," and, "I want to eat a burrito!"

Lynda had an idea what these references were. "Flying kites" sounded pretty similar to "getting high." And she was pretty sure that a "burrito" was actually a joint. Scrolling through the messages, Lynda couldn't believe how far back in time these conversations about marijuana went! She had no idea that her son had been using drugs for such a long time. How had she been so blind? She needed to wrap her head around all of the signs that were there, but that she had missed.

Okay, her son was doing drugs. She needed to accept that, even though she didn't want to. Lynda was smart enough to know that ignoring the problem would not make it magically disappear. She had to do something. But, what?

She continued perusing the Twitter messages, this time paying more attention to the Twitter handles. When Lynda tapped on the handle, it took her to that person's account. That was interesting; she was able to see a good deal of information, and that often included the user's real name.

Some of the names she recognized. After all, she had known most of Ben's friends since they were in elementary school together. These kids had slept at her house, attended birthday parties together, and played on the same basketball team. She knew most of the parents, too, but not all.

Were they all smoking pot together? How was that possible? They were good kids! These were the athletes and the top students. When they came to her home they always said, "Yes ma'am," and, "No ma'am." Lynda couldn't believe for a second that they were using drugs.

At this point, Lynda had discovered some drug related messages on an iPod, names of some kids that she knew, and some she didn't, and one incident of her son sneaking out in the middle of the night and being brought home by the local cops. Lynda considered what this could mean. She knew that throughout time, teenagers have always done things they shouldn't do; experimenting with alcohol and drugs, and pushing the limits. She also knew that teens thought they knew so much more than they actually did.

Ben had often made comments times about how a particular rule at school was "stupid," so in his mind he didn't have to follow it. Lynda was sure that he held to a similar philosophy when it came to the laws which declared that marijuana is an illegal substance. In his mind it should be completely legal for all kinds of use. As of right now, the autumn of 2013, in the state of Texas, using marijuana was against the law. If he were caught by the police with pot in his possession, there would be legal consequences.

She could imagine him saying, "But, Officer, this is really a stupid law. There's nothing wrong with pot! People become violent when they drink alcohol, not when they smoke pot. Just let me go home, so I can get high, okay?"

Lynda laughed out loud, picturing that.

She realized that many people today did not see this as a black-and-white issue. There were a lot of grey areas. Colorado and Washington legalized the recreational use of marijuana in November of 2012. There were still many regulations, of course, including the fact that it's illegal for minors to use or purchase it. But in her son's mind, as well as many others, this was the first step toward nationwide legalization, so all of the existing laws could be thrown out the window.

She didn't doubt that marijuana would be legalized throughout the United States at some point, and regulated in a similar way that alcohol is regulated. But at this particular time and location, it's still illegal to use it for either recreational or medicinal purposes. Besides that, it was against Lynda's own house rules for her son to be using drugs. Obviously, he didn't respect that. So, there needed to be consequences.

Ben, James and Matt were sitting in a circle on the floor of James' room, passing around a bong. It was Ben's turn. The water in the bong bubbled brightly as he inhaled. The room was dark, with the blinds closed tightly. The only light came from the partially open closet door. Bright LED light was streaming through the gap.

That day, James had revealed his indoor grow to his friends. It took up the majority of his small closet, which was fine, since his clothes were stuffed in a six-drawer dresser in his room.

"Come on, man," said James. "PPP."

"I thought that only applied to joints," replied Ben, as he handed the bong to his friend.

"Nope. 'Puff, puff, pass' applies to everything."

Ben was impressed. James was a true marijuana connoisseur. He knew all the lingo, and he understood the subtle differences between the many different varieties of weed. He had even built the hydroponic system that maintained the pot plants in the closet. It was a complex system of PVC, plastic buckets and LED lighting that required no soil or sunlight. The plants were huge and plentiful. It was a perfect setup.

James was a brilliant young man who could build practically anything he could dream of. When he was younger he excelled in math and science. These days, as a sophomore in high school, he was squeaking by with Cs, and the occasional D thrown in. But if he thought of something innovative that had to do with smoking as much pot as possible, then he put his all into it.

Now it was Matt's turn with the bong.

"Dude, I can't believe that you have that thing in your closet. How do your parents not know?" he asked.

"They're gone pretty much all the time," James explained. "They're both doctors and they work a lot. They never come in my room. They are all about giving me my privacy." He grinned. "And that is just fine with me."

"Oh, you're so lucky," said Ben. "My mom goes to work during the day, but other than that she's around all the time." It was his turn again, and he happily inhaled.

James' doctor parents were "free-range" parents. They believed that children learned how to take care of themselves by giving them complete independence. There was no supervision for James, and no discipline. While a certain level of independence and learning lessons on their own is definitely a good thing for teenagers, taking it to the extreme is asking for trouble. The same can be said for helicopter parents. Anything that is taken to the extreme is a recipe for disaster. Good parenting consists of a combination of micromanaging your children, and letting them run amok.

But James' parents were afraid of inhibiting him with too much structure and stifling his creativity by imposing rules on him. So, while they're working long shifts at the hospital two miles away, and traveling to Houston for medical conferences, James is making sure that his marijuana plants are healthy and growing.

"Have you guys ever tried dabs?" James asked.

The two boys shook their heads.

"Total THC extraction," James explained. "You end up

with this waxy stuff that's really potent. It gets you really high, really fast."

He continued to explain to his audience that creating dabs was a way to utilize the remainder of the plant, after you smoked the buds. The THC was extracted from the leftover leaves and stems.

Ben was stoked. He was always on the lookout for new ways to get high, and this sounded like a great plan.

"We should totally do that!" said Ben. "When and where?"

"Next weekend my parents are going out of town for a medical conference. We can do it then," said James. His parents trusted him completely, and they saw no need to have anyone stay with him when they left town for business purposes.

"Awesome, it's a plan," said Ben. He could hardly wait for next weekend. Ben was fairly ignorant when it came to the terminology of his new-found hobby. If someone used a word he didn't know, he just pretended that he did. Usually, someone would offer a definition and he didn't end up looking stupid.

The three boys spent the remainder of the afternoon getting stoned and playing Super Mario Brothers on the Wii. The images on the screen appeared extraordinarily vivid to Ben, but for some reason he kept losing his virtual life.

The room was smoky and reeked of that unmistakable marijuana smell. It wasn't as bad as it could have been. James had a state-of-the-art ionic air purifier, and that seemed to help lessen the odor.

"Can you guys stay over tonight?" asked James. "We can get a couple pizzas. My mom left her credit card."

Ben thought that was really cool; his mother didn't believe in using credit cards. If she didn't have the cash to pay for an item, she didn't buy it. Using a credit card felt like having access to free money. This was going to be a great night! Pizza, video games, and weed. What could be better?

"I just can't understand why people have such a problem with weed," Ben remarked. "It's not dangerous; you never meet an 'angry stoner' but 'angry drunks' are all over the place!"

"I know, man, you're preaching to the choir," said James. "I'll never get why it isn't legal all over the country. It's like a miracle drug."

"I know, right?" exclaimed Ben. He was getting excited now. When he was discussing the many virtues of marijuana he was in his element. And he was so thrilled to have found a kindred spirit in James. Matt was happy to get high with him once in a while, but Ben and James were on the same sheet of music. They both understood that not only was pot not dangerous, it was probably the cure for cancer.

It was ridiculous that pot was still illegal. And because the boys really believed that this particular law was wrong, they also believed that it didn't apply to them. They knew better than the police and the legislators. They were above it.

Lynda was fixing a spinach and goat cheese omelet for herself when her youngest son walked through the doorway. It was dinner time, and she was hungry. She would fix a tomato salad to accompany her omelet, and she'd be all set.

"Hi Mom," said Ben as he brushed past her. He was noticeably avoiding eye contact.

"Ben, wait," said Lynda. "I want to talk to you." She reached for his arm, in order to bring him closer to him. He jerked away.

"No, I'm in a hurry. I'm spending the night at a friend's house."

He still wouldn't look at her.

"You've been out all day. You don't need to go anywhere tonight." That made him look at her. His eyes were completely bloodshot and swollen along his lower lids.

"Oh my god, you're stoned again!" She was shocked. What was going on? She had always talked to him about the dangers of drugs, and she had certainly never had marijuana in the house. Where was he getting it?

Ben turned away from her and started walking upstairs. She stepped into his path.

"I'm talking to you!" she said in a firm voice that wasn't quite yelling. Lynda believed in staying in control as much as possible. Once you start yelling, you've pretty much lost any control you've had.

"Mom, I really don't care," he said. "I'm getting some things, and I'm spending the night at a friend's house."

"No, you're not. You're staying home tonight!"

She was forced to look up at him, in order to gaze into his bloodshot eyes. He once again tried to go around her. Lynda stepped along with him, into the path he was trying to take; upstairs to his room to gather some overnight things. She stepped in front of him.

He let out a frustrated groan, and his fist flashed away from his body. It hit the wall with a loud "thump!" and the drywall crumbled inward.

"Mom, you need to get out of my way!" Ben said, and he placed his hand on her shoulder, and shoved her aside. He took the stairs two at a time and disappeared.

Lynda was shocked; she stared disbelieving at the hole in the wall of the hallway. She was stunned that her son put his hands on her, and actually pushed her out of his way! Along with the outrage she felt, there was an inkling of fear. He stood about six inches taller than her, and he outweighed her by about thirty pounds. Would he actually harm her? She really didn't think so. She knew that he loved her; they had always had a close mother-son relationship.

But, during the past few months, there was no denying that he had changed. She had attributed the changes to his age, and the hormones that were certainly rushing through him. Boys could be just as emotional as girls! Now, with the knowledge that he was doing drugs in conjunction with the normal teenage drama, Lynda was hesitant to push too hard. She really didn't know what he was capable of.

Would he actually strike her? If he felt badgered and provoked, would he turn violent?

A door slammed upstairs, and Ben came racing down the staircase. He did not look at or speak to his mother as he passed her. One more door slammed as he left the house, and Lynda stood in silent wonder.

She wondered what had happened to her sweet little boy. She wondered where she had gone wrong with parenting him. She wondered why he felt the need to turn to drugs, and disrespect her so blatantly. She wondered what would happen now. Most of all, she wondered what in the world she was going to do.

Saturday Evening

Lynda realized that she couldn't run after Ben and drag him back to the house. There were only so many things she could control, and her son's whereabouts were not one of those things right now.

She remembered her dinner that was still sitting on the kitchen island. She really was hungry, so she pulled a stool up to the countertop. She was about to dig in when she realized that a glass of wine would be a great accompaniment to the omelet, and it would certainly help calm her down a bit. A half-full bottle of Malbec was in the pantry. She poured a glass and was about to sit back down when a thought occurred to her.

"I'll grab that iPod and go through it a bit more closely while I'm eating." Always a fan of multi-tasking, Lynda went upstairs to her room. The iPod was still in the safe, of course. Ben did not have the combination, and she doubted that he realized it was missing.

At the foot of the stairs she passed by the fist-sized hole in the wall. She shuddered involuntarily. What was this man-child capable of?

Finally, she was ready to sit down and enjoy her cold omelet, and room-temperature wine. Oh, and she remembered that she was going to whip up a quick tomato salad. The recipe, if you could call it that, came from her parents. She grabbed two Roma tomatoes, and sliced them very thinly. That was easy to do, because she kept her Henckels knives ridiculously sharp. She tossed the sliced tomatoes in a bowl and added a just a bit of salt and pepper, a couple spoonfuls of olive oil, and some chopped fresh parsley.

Her parents were originally from Germany and this was a favorite salad that they served frequently. Lynda always thought that simple food is the best. You don't need a lot of fancy ingredients to create a delicious meal; just a few fresh, high-quality items and you were good to go.

Throughout her childhood, Lynda always made sure that she did what her parents expected of her. She knew that if she was told to be home by 11:00, she better be home by 11:00. If she brought home a C, she knew she was going to get it.

It wasn't necessarily that she feared the punishment itself. Lynda was deathly afraid of disappointing her mom. As a young girl and even as a teenager, the worst words in the world were, "I'm not mad at you. I'm disappointed in you."

The result was that teenaged Lynda didn't get into a whole lot of trouble. Her grades were pretty consistent As and Bs, she was home for dinner most nights, and her bed was always made. Lynda did not talk back to her parents, even when they were blatantly wrong about something. Her mom would tell you that she wasn't prejudiced, but she had a not very nice nickname for a Jewish boy that Lynda dated in college. Lynda kept her mouth shut.

Occasionally she had attended a party in high school where someone had brought beer, but the most she would have was one, if even that. Back then, she wasn't really a fan of beer. The only choices were Bud and Coors; the tasty microbrews weren't available until years later. Yes, she admitted it freely, she was a beer snob.

She hung out with the nerds when she was young, which by association indicated that's what she was probably known as. That didn't mean they were all a bunch of saints, but she really couldn't remember pot being part of their weekend activities. Her group would go to the movies, and the high school football games.

And in the back of her mind, there was always the thought of her mom and how disappointed she would be if she were to experiment with any type of drug.

Lynda was never a sports kid or a band kid when she was in school, but she kept herself busy with a part-time job since she was fifteen. Several nights a week and most weekends were spent seating restaurant patrons at the Dragon Palace. The food was great and the owner was crazy. There were many nights when he yelled at a customer when they had a small complaint. Luckily, these were the days before Yelp reviews.

She remembered a couple of stoners from high school. There were just a few. She didn't know them well, but she knew who they were. They hung out in the smoking area behind the building. They sat in the back of the class, and didn't participate in the discussions. She never actually saw them getting high, but everyone just knew that they were the pot heads, the losers, the kids who really didn't give a crap about anything except getting high.

Lynda broke from reminiscing about her high school days. She picked up the iPod and tapped the Twitter application. She knew that she would find a ton of messages regarding "flying kites," "eating burritos," and more euphemisms for smoking joints. What she was looking for was any name that she recognized. She was looking for clues as to which kids were her son's party buddies.

Even though the kids used Twitter handles, they often put some form of their actual name in the profile, and this information was displayed. She saw two names that she recognized; Matt Martinez and Brad Carmichael. Both of these boys had gone to school with Ben since first grade.

Lynda knew Matt's mother, Dottie, fairly well. She was associated with Brad's mom only in passing. They would see each other at school functions, but that had mostly been during the boys' elementary school days. Once they started middle school, parent involvement in the regular school day lessened quite a bit.

The summer that the boys were all in fifth grade together, Matt practically lived at Lynda's house. There were countless sleepovers. Those boys used to stay up until 4:00 in the morning playing video games and eating pizza. Lynda had no problem with that. She loved having them at her home.

During that summer Lynda and Dottie got to know each other. Dottie would often come in for a glass of wine when she dropped off Matt, and the two women chatted on the back patio for a few minutes. Dottie was a stay-at-home-mom, who had a little Scentsy business on the side. Lynda had hosted several parties for Dottie over the years. There were decorative wax warmers in several rooms in her home.

She even hosted a Scentsy party at her office a couple of Christmases ago, and that was a success for everyone. It made gift shopping easy for her coworkers, many of whom were men, and had no clue what to buy for their wives and girlfriends. Dottie was who Lynda called if it started storming just as school was getting out, and she couldn't pick Ben up. Dottie was always happy to give him a ride home, or even let him hang out at her house for a while.

And now, Lynda needed to call Dottie and ask if she was aware that their sons were probably getting high together on a semi-regular basis. This is not a phone call she's looking forward to.

Dottie answered the phone on the second ring.

"Hey, Lynda, how are you?" her voice was cheery; it sounded like she was genuinely happy to hear from Lynda. "It's been a long time! What do you need, honey, some more wax melts? Or another party?" Dottie was getting excited now.

"Hi, Dottie," said Lynda. "No I don't need anything Scentsy. I'm calling about Matt and Ben. I think they've been spending a lot of time together lately. Do you know what they've been doing?"

"No, I haven't seen either of them a whole lot lately. What's going on?"

Lynda gave her friend a quick summary of the latest events that had been occurring with Ben. She told her about the iPod, and about finding the incriminating messages.

"According to the Twitter messages I've seen, it looks like Matt and a few other boys are all involved in getting high with Ben."

Dottie was silent for a moment. When she spoke the tone of her voice had changed. She wasn't quite as cheery as when she had first answered the phone.

"You know that Matt's life revolves around football and wrestling. There's a zero-tolerance policy on both teams. I really don't think he's doing any kind of drugs."

"I never would have thought that any of the boys would do this," said Lynda. "But the messages I saw really sound like that's what's going on." She paused. Dottie didn't reply.

"I'm so sorry," said Lynda. "I hate to be the one to give you this news. What I'd like to do is work together, and try to figure out how we can help the boys."

"Lynda," began Dottie, "I'm really sorry if Ben is getting into drugs. That's a really hard thing to deal with, especially with his father not in the picture. But I guarantee that Matt is not involved in this. He's a good boy. "

"Of course he's a good boy. They're both good boys," Lynda was getting a little irritated now.

"I know they are," Dottie replied quickly. "And I know my son. He is not involved in any kind of drug use."

Her voice softened a little. "I'm sorry that you're going through this. Let me know if your office would like to have another party. I'll talk to you later."

Lynda stared at the phone in her hand, stunned. Well, maybe not completely stunned. She acknowledged that this was one reason she was so nervous about calling other parents. She knew that some parents would blame her son and believe that he was the instigator, and some would refuse to believe that their own children could possibly be involved in drugs, like Dottie just had.

If a parent other than Lynda had been the one to discover the pot smoking, Lynda would want that parent to call her! She had often heard other parents say, "Oh, I know my child very well. If he were using drugs, I would know it!" Lynda wasn't so sure about that. There are certainly physical symptoms that indicate drug use; a child's personality can change, too. But it isn't as easy as some parents might think.

She thought about this, as she took a bite of her dinner. Should she have suspected that something was going on with Ben sooner? Were there signs that she had missed? Teenagers are supposed to pull away from their parents. It's part of growing up. No matter how much she had wanted her teenaged-baby-boy to hang out with her and watch TV, he preferred to hang out in his bedroom. Lynda got that. She remembered being the same way.

When Lynda was in high school she would stay up until three in the morning reading Stephen King novels. That was both good and bad. Although she loved stories like Carrie and The Stand, she remembered reading Salem's Lot in the middle of the night, staring at the window, waiting for a cute little blond vampire to scratch on the glass and try to enter the house.

So, she understood where he was coming from. But now, looking back, was it a sign? The pulling away from her, and wanting to be alone? It was impossible to know for sure. How much of his behavior was just normal, moody teenage crap, and how much was due to the pot?

Lynda began dialing the number of the next person on her list. The phone was answered after two rings.

"Hello, this is Kathy."

"Hi Kathy, this is Lynda Murphy, Ben's mom."

"Oh, hi, Lynda! How are you?"

"I'm fine, thanks." She took a sip of wine. "I'm calling because I need to talk to you about our boys. I've found some evidence that shows they're probably doing drugs together."

"Oh my gosh!" exclaimed Kathy. She sounded stunned, and genuinely concerned. Lynda felt hopeful! Finally, a parent who understood the severity of the situation.

"I've been afraid that something like this might happen. None of our kids are safe from this," said Kathy.

Lynda felt a wave of relief flood through her. She had found an ally in Kathy Carmichael.

"Kathy, I'm so happy to hear you say that. I just got off the phone with another mom who refused to believe that her son was involved. We need to work together to help our boys."

"I agree completely!" said Kathy. "We have to make sure they don't ruin their lives! What do you think they've been getting into? Cocaine? Heroin? Oh, God, I hope it's not meth. I've heard so many horror stories about kids getting into meth."

"Oh, no!" replied Lynda. "It's nothing like that, as far as I know. I found messages that show they've been smoking a lot of pot."

The other end of the line was silent. Lynda actually counted to seven before Kathy spoke.

"Pot?" she said. "They're smoking pot?"

"Yes, according to the messages I found, it looks like they're doing it a lot. Ben snuck out of the house the other night, and the police called me."

"Pot," said Kathy. "Lynda, all teenagers smoke pot. Pot isn't a problem! Didn't you smoke pot when you were in high school? I know I did!"

"No, actually, I didn't," replied Lynda. "But I don't think that really matters. The point is that the kids should not be spending all of their time trying to find a way to get high."

"Oh, they're not spending all their time getting high. They're just boys. Lynda, if you had told me that they were using coke or meth, or even pills, then I would have been concerned. But it's pot! Pot has been around forever. This really isn't anything to worry about."

"Don't you care that it's illegal?"

Kathy replied with a laugh.

"Oh, come on. It's illegal right now, but we know that's going to change. It's a stupid law. Listen, if you come across anything serious, let me know. I really want to know, Lynda. I'm not that mom who thinks that her son is perfect, and can do no wrong. But pot is not a problem. You have a good night."

Lynda stared at the phone in her hand. It's just pot? Really? She was shocked. She could not believe that Kathy was being so cavalier about this! Would Kathy feel the same way if the boys were getting drunk all the time? Maybe.

So far, she was zero for two. She was on her own.

Lynda cleaned up her dinner dishes and thought about what to do.

Kathy didn't seem to care that marijuana is illegal in Texas. Lynda wondered what the police had to say about that. She grabbed the iPod and her keys, and headed to the police station.

Saturday Night

The police station was only a couple of miles from Lynda's home, in the downtown section of the small Texas town she lived in. Actually, like many suburban towns across the county, it wasn't as small as it used to be. Rosemeade had already grown tremendously since she had moved there eight years ago. New subdivisions and McMansions were popping up all over the place.

She pulled into a parking space, grabbed the iPod, and walked in the front door of the station. The building was newer; it was nothing like the inner-city police stations that she saw on TV and in the movies. The lobby was quiet and dimly lit; Lynda thought it was kind of like walking into a spa.

She had expected a little more activity. No one was sitting on the polished benches, no one was walking hurriedly by. Apparently, eight o'clock on a Saturday night was not a busy time for the Rosemeade PD. Unless, of course, the action was happening in another part of the building.

A police officer sat at a greeter's desk behind a tall glass partition. Lynda assumed, correctly, that the glass was bullet proof.

She was nervous. Lynda had never had much interaction

with the police throughout her life. Sure, she had been pulled over a few times, but it was never anything serious. She wasn't really afraid; in her mind, police officers were there to help, not to hurt her. Nothing had ever happened in her small world to disprove that theory, so that was what she believed.

"Hello," she said.

"Hi there," said the officer. He smiled at her warmly. That made her think of the character, "Officer Friendly" she had learned about as a child. Teaching school children via coloring books and comic strips that as a whole, the police department was there to help you.

This officer was in his early forties, like Lynda. He had dark hair, and nice eyes that crinkled around the edges when he smiled at her. The name plate pinned to his uniform said, "Officer Roy Hughes."

"How can I help you?" he asked.

"Well, I have a few questions. I found this iPod in my son's room, and there are messages showing that he and his friends have been using drugs. I'd like to know what I can do about it." That was it in a nutshell. What could Lynda do about it? Could she do anything?

She gave him the iPod, so he could see the messages for himself. He scrolled through, reading them.

"Do you know any of these kids?" he asked.

"Yes, I do, and I called two of the moms just before I came here. One refused to believe that her son is involved with drugs, and the other one thinks pot isn't a big deal, and we should just let it go."

The officer chuckled. "You'd be surprised how many people believe that. Now, I'm not saying that marijuana should or shouldn't be legal. That's not my call. But right now, here in Texas and lot of other places in the country, it's illegal, and there are consequences for possession."

Lynda understood that completely. It didn't matter if you agree with the principles behind a particular law. If you break that law there will be consequences.

"What can happen to a teenager if they're caught with it?" she asked.

"That depends on a few things," he said. "If they're caught with pot on any public property, like a school, a church, or a city park, it immediately becomes a felony charge. Also, if a teenager is hanging out smoking pot and they see the cops coming, what do you think they're going to do?"

"Take off running," Lynda replied.

"Exactly," said Officer Hughes. "And that becomes 'evading an officer.' The charges can quickly become more serious." He paused for a moment.

"You really don't want your son to get involved with the law. Having a record is not a good way for him to start his adult life."

"But if he's caught by the police it might wake him up. Wouldn't that be a good thing?"

"I think the negatives would really outweigh the benefits. You should avoid that if possible."

"Okay. Where are the kids getting the pot?" Lynda wanted to know.

"Dealers from Dallas are bringing it out to the suburbs. Rosemeade, Plano, and Frisco have pretty affluent residents. The dealers know that if they bring it, it will sell. Or, people are growing it in their homes."

"You're kidding?" Lynda found that hard to believe. She thought that just happened in the rundown, inner-city neighborhoods.

"Oh no, you can find indoor growing systems all over the Internet. They can even be contained in a large crate, so you can't tell what it is just by looking at it from the outside. It has a hydroponic system inside, so the plants don't need soil to grow. And the lights are LEDs; no sunlight required."

"And people are doing that right here in Rosemeade?"

"Oh, yeah. We get tips once in a while of a marijuana grow in someone's house. If you hear of anything, we'd like to know about it."

Lynda looked at Officer Hughes. He had provided some very interesting information, but she still didn't have a plan for moving forward.

"What can I do to help my son?" she asked. "I'm worried that he's going to lose motivation for anything else but getting high, I'm afraid that he'll get in trouble with the law, and I'm afraid of things that I don't even know about yet! I have to do something to help him, and I have no idea what that is."

Roy Hughes sighed. He was glad she had come to the station, and he really wanted to help her. He could tell that she was a concerned mother who genuinely wanted to help her son.

Unfortunately, the truth was that marijuana was rampant in the affluent suburbs of Dallas, just like every other suburban area in America. The dealers wanted to sell their wares to whomever had the money to buy. Very often, the most loyal customers were high school and college students who lived on the outskirts of the larger cities.

He chose to explain to her what she could do, as opposed to all the things that she could not control.

"You know," he began, "parents have a lot more control over teenagers than they realize."

Lynda looked at him skeptically.

"It's true. It's still legal to spank your kids."

Lynda laughed at that.

"He's quite a bit taller than I am," she said. "I doubt that I'd be very effective."

"Well, it is legal. And it's completely illegal for him to touch you. We had a situation once where a teenager called Child Protective Services, and said that his dad was abusing him. It was a load of crap, but once CPS gets a call, they have to look into it. He ended up having to take parenting classes. Do you know what he did wrong?"

Lynda shook her head.

"He opened the door and let them into his home," said Officer Hughes. "CPS doesn't have the right to just come into your house and start interrogating you. Just take their business card, and tell them that your lawyer will call them the next day."

"Really? I always thought they were so powerful."

"They like to think they are. I've see so many screw-ups caused by CPS. Different representatives will give different instructions to parents, and it gets very confusing. Don't deal with them without an attorney."

"Okay, that's really good to know," said Lynda.

"Yeah, that kid who called CPS on his dad really needed a good spanking. He was a mess. The dad told me that his son did try to hit him a few times. Luckily, he was able to get out of the way."

"I worry about that," Lynda told him. "It's never happened before, but he's so much stronger than I am. If he's mad enough, I don't know what he might do."

"If he ever does lay a hand on you, that's when you should call 911," said Officer Hughes. "That is illegal."

"You want me to call the police on my son?" Lynda was having a hard time with this.

"Officer," she said. "This is my baby. He's my youngest child. I can't imagine calling the police on him."

"You know, I get that. I have kids, too. No parent wants to have to get this tough." Officer Hughes paused. He knew that Lynda was an attractive single mom, who just wanted the best for her son. That's why she was here on a Saturday night, instead of out partying with her friends.

"Look," he said, "If I can help you in any way, please call." He hesitated for a moment, then smiled. "You know, you can handcuff him to his bed if you need to. That way you'll know where he is."

Lynda burst out laughing. "Too bad I don't have any handcuffs!"

"Hold on a minute. I can probably fix that."

Officer Hughes disappeared through a doorway that was hidden behind the desk. It was like one of the hidden doorways that blended into the walls in the White House. Lynda never liked those doors. In her opinion doors should be doors and walls should be walls. What was the point in merging the two?

He came back about a minute later.

"Here," he said. He placed a set of handcuffs and a key on the counter in front of her.

"These might help," he said. "If you need to use them, go ahead."

"Uh.....okay," said Lynda. "I don't know if I can do that." She looked at the metal in front of her; the rings and the chain that connected them. Really? She was expected to slap these cuffs on her baby in order to keep tabs on him?

"You bet. Cuff him to his bed frame, so you know where he is." He sounded serious, but when Lynda looked at him, his eyes were laughing. She decided to call his bluff.

"I think I will take them," she said. "They just might come in handy."

"Good! Okay, one more thing I want to make sure you understand. As the parent of a minor, you technically own everything that he has. That includes his clothing, electronics, and even any money that he earns. If he refuses to follow your rules, you could take all of those things and make his life pretty uncomfortable."

"That's true," she replied. Lynda was familiar with the tough love philosophy. Some parents even went to the extent of taking a disobedient child's bedroom door off the hinges. Goodbye, privacy!

Lynda really didn't want to have to resort to those tactics. She wanted to have a good relationship with her son, not a contentious one. But, she also knew that it wasn't her job to be his friend. Ben had plenty of friends. She is his mother, and that's a completely different role.

Officer Hughes handed her his business card.

"I mean it," he said. "Call me if you need help."

"Thanks. I appreciate all of your time tonight."

She pocketed the business card, and put the handcuffs in her purse. The sky was dark when she walked outside; Lynda had been inside talking to Officer Hughes for quite a while. She wouldn't be too upset if she had the chance to talk with him again sometime, when the subject wasn't her crazy teenager.

The house was dark as she pulled into her parking spot

out front. She had hoped that it would be illuminated, indicating that Ben was home. Unfortunately, she wouldn't see him until the following evening.

Sunday Afternoon

Matt was carrying the large box of groceries for his mom. Geez, it was heavy. When Costco gives you a box for your groceries, they make sure it's packed as full as possible. Then his mom made sure that he was around to carry it inside.

He placed the box on the kitchen island with a loud thunk, then grabbed the cucumber, bell peppers and the clamshell package of baby spinach. Time for a salad.

"Matt, before you eat please put the rest of the groceries away," Dottie asked as she entered the kitchen from the garage.

"Mom, I'll do it after I eat," said Matt.

"No, you'll put the groceries away first. Your stomach will survive."

"Ugh!"

"Yeah, I know, you have it so bad here," Dottie was smiling. "Don't worry, I'll help you."

Matt smiled. "Okay, thanks Mom," he said.

Dottie was hefting two gallons of milk into the refrigerator when she remembered the call from Lynda the day before.

"Hey, I got the strangest call yesterday from Ben's mother," she said to her son. "Do you still do things together?"

Matt was nervous. Why was Ben's mother calling his mom? The only time he hung out with Ben anymore was to get high. Granted, that had been quite often lately, but it was all they did together. Did Mrs. Murphy know? Did she tell his mom? What other reason would she have to make that phone call?

He tried to control his voice as he answered.

"Uh, yeah, we still hang out. We go skateboarding sometimes, or play video games," Matt told her.

"Okay," Dottie replied. "Hmm, I think I'll make this pork tenderloin for dinner. Does that sound good? We can grill it, with garlic and lime."

"Sure, Mom," said Matt. She didn't appear too concerned about how he and Ben had been spending their time together, if she was thinking about what to cook for dinner. But, then again, his mom was always thinking about the meal that she was going to cook next. She was a cooking and baking fiend. This was fine with Matt, since most teenage boys can consume enough food to force their parents to declare bankruptcy. Matt burned so many calories playing football and baseball that he might even eat more than the average teenage boy. He had no problem with his mother's mini-obsession about cooking.

"Anyway," Dottie continued, "Mrs. Murphy called me yesterday and told me that she thinks you and Ben are doing drugs together! Can you believe that? I told her, 'Absolutely not! My son would never do drugs!'"

Matt's mouth had gone dry; his face felt hot. He turned away from his mother, to make sure she couldn't see him. He was sure that his face was a dead giveaway and she would instantly know the truth if she looked at him.

He knew she was waiting for an answer from him. He breathed deeply, and did his best to compose himself.

"I don't know why she would think that," said Matt. He felt that his voice was shaky. Had his mom picked up on that?

"Well, that's what I told her," replied Dottie.

Matt felt relief wash over him. He gathered the veggies for his salad and commenced chopping the cucumbers and peppers.

"Do we have salad dressing?" Matt asked his mom.

"I think we're out. You'll need to make some." Dottie didn't buy salad dressing at the store. She saw no need. They were filled with who knew what kinds of preservatives that allowed those bottles to sit on the shelves for months.

So, Matt grabbed the gallon of olive oil, balsamic vinegar and a variety of spices to create his mom's version of balsamic vinaigrette. He grabbed what he called the "stick blender" and emulsified the concoction. Perfect.

"I'm going to eat in my room, Mom," he called over his shoulder as he walked down the hall.

"Sure, don't worry, I'll clean up your mess!" She really didn't mind. Dottie realized that one day, very soon, he wouldn't be leaving messes in her kitchen. Matt had a lot of great opportunities ahead of him. Although his grades were pretty average, he was an excellent athlete. He would certainly earn a full scholarship based on either football or baseball. They were counting on it; there wasn't any extra money for college for him.

But, the way he had talked to her about the phone call with Ben's mom nagged at her. She had made an effort to watch him during that conversation. She noticed that he wasn't looking at her, which was odd. His voice, when he talked to her, was almost quavering. It wasn't anything she could really put her finger on, and say, "I know you're lying to me because your nose is twitching!" It was a feeling she had.

How accurate is a mother's intuition? How true are feelings? Throughout the years Dottie had learned that if her gut was trying to tell her something, she should listen. Years ago, she had been engaged to her high school sweetheart. They were both still in college at Texas A&M, and he was pushing hard for them to marry.

At the time she thought it was romantic. "Oh, he wants me all to himself, he loves me so much!" And yet, there was something in the back of her mind, in her gut, that told her not to go through with it. She didn't.

She'll never forget the night that she broke it off with him for good. Sure, the whole relationship was on-again, off-again, but the night that she told him that it was definitely over, was not pretty.

Dottie was living in the dorm at the time, and her boyfriend lived in a fraternity house. He had come to her dorm room because she had told him that they needed to talk. At that time, he was too young to realize that any time a woman (mother, girlfriend, teacher, or boss) uttered the words, "We need to talk," indicated that something unpleasant was about to happen.

When he arrived at her dorm room he reached for her and tried to kiss her, which was his usual way of greeting his girlfriend. She turned away and asked him to sit down. Dottie began to explain that they were both very young, still had several years of school to go, and neither one of them knew where they would end up after graduation.

While she cared for him deeply, she thought it was best for both of them if they break up.

He went ballistic.

He started screaming at her, swearing and calling her filthy names. He picked up items from her desk and hurled them at the wall. The alarm clock exploded into tiny pieces.

The door to the dorm room burst open, and two guys grabbed Dottie's now ex-boyfriend. The resident assistant was behind them. Oh, thank God she had called for help! The two men who had a grip on the ex ushered him out of the room. He was still yelling at the top of his voice, saying, "I'll get you for this! You're gonna pay!"

She never heard from him again.

Reflecting on that day, Dottie remembered the feeling she had always had when she was with him. Doubt. Uncertainty. Knowing that something was wrong, but not being able to put her finger on it.

That's how she felt now after talking to Matt. Or, rather, after not getting an answer from him. A non-talkative teenager is nothing out of the ordinary. Teenagers have been ignoring their parents since the dawn of time. But something just didn't feel right with that conversation. He wouldn't even look at her; Dottie believed that he had gone out of his way to turn around and avoid her gaze, just so she couldn't see his face. It wasn't like him.

Dottie hated to consider this, but was Lynda right? Were Matt and Ben doing drugs together? No, she couldn't believe that. She wouldn't believe it. Matt is your typical All-American athlete; he knows that the school and the team incorporate a zero-tolerance policy when it comes to drug use. If the school learns of any infraction, he would be off the team. She knew that sports were everything to him. He knew that his future depended upon athletics, and his ability to receive an athletic-related scholarship.

She couldn't believe that Matt would jeopardize his future. But still….she had that funny feeling in her gut. Something was not right.

Should she drug test him herself? Dottie knew that home tests were available online, or even at the local drug store. She could get in her car right now and drive to Walgreens to pick up a kit. If she did this, and the test results were positive, then Dottie would have the opportunity to attack this problem head-on. She would work with her son, and care for him, and make sure he got the help he needed.

But, come on, he wasn't doing drugs. She was 99.9% sure of it.

Dottie slammed the side of the knife blade against a clove of garlic, peeled it, and chopped it into tiny pieces. She began to forget all about Lynda Murphy and marijuana.

Matt tried to eat his salad, but it was hard; sweat was pouring down his face. When he was stressed, that's what happened. He was terrified that his mom would find out that he'd been smoking pot with Ben. Matt wasn't even sure why he started. He couldn't really call it peer pressure. Ben really didn't have much influence over him. Was it boredom? That could have been it.

Since he started spending time with Ben, he'd began losing interest in some of the things he used to do. Sure, he still loved sports and was still an excellent athlete. But given the choice between going for a run with his dad and getting high with Ben, he'd been choosing getting high.

Matt wasn't even sure why he had started. Boredom? That was possible. He remembered that first night, when he had run into Ben, James, and a few other kids at the park. He hadn't spent time with this group in ages; they used to be so close in elementary school, and seeing them again caused him to feel a little nostalgic.

Maybe that was the reason; nostalgia. Maybe he wanted a way to reconnect with his old friends, and regain some of those childhood connections.

Whatever the reason, he was hooked now. He found himself thinking about it all the time. He would be in school, or trying to study, and he'd start thinking about getting high. Matt did not purchase the pot himself; he left that to Ben. Because of that, he didn't think he had a problem. He wasn't buying; he didn't know any dealers.

But he really wanted to smoke; bad.

He sent Ben a text:

Matt: Hey what are you doing?

Ben: Hanging with James. Wanna come?

Matt: Yeah.

Ben: Okay bring $20.

Matt: Okay.

Matt never had a problem getting his hands on a few dollars. His mom was very happy to throw money at him. In Dottie's opinion it was Matt's job to do well in school and in sports. At this point in his life it wasn't necessary for him to work. He'll be doing plenty of that in the future. So, as long as he was doing what he needed to do, his mom gave him money for going out with his friends. No questions asked.

She was still preparing dinner when Matt walked into the kitchen.

"Hey, Mom, can I have $20? I'm going to meet some friends and get something to eat," he said.

"Honey, dinner is just in a few hours. I want you here, and I want you to eat with us," replied his mom.

"Oh, don't worry," he grinned. "I can always eat. But I'd like to hang with my friends for a little bit."

"Okay, there's a twenty in my purse. Be back by 5:00."

"Thanks Mom." He grabbed the money, and gave her a quick kiss on the cheek on his way out the door.

Sunday Evening

Lynda didn't see Ben until Sunday evening. She had decided that she would spend the weekend just like she always did; doing house projects, grocery shopping, and running. She could have spent the entire time worrying about Ben, trying to track him down.

Of course, Lynda was concerned about her son; she wanted to help her son and get him back on track. But she also realized that she should not worry about things that she could not control. Worrying didn't solve anything; it just made her crazy.

So, she kept herself busy all weekend, waiting for Ben to come home. She knew that he had to show up at some point; where else would he go? Lynda highly doubted that her son would be welcome in the home of one of his friends. He occasionally mentioned moving out to stay with a friend for an extended period of time. He was delusional!

What parent would want someone else's teenager living with them? If Ben were truly living in a dangerous situation, that would be a different story. But there's no way anyone could ever say that Lynda was not a fit mother. She provided absolutely everything that Ben needed, and many things that he wanted.

She knew that Ben thought he had it pretty rough at her house. In his mind he was the victim. He truly believed that if he pleaded his case to his friends' parents, they would certainly take pity on him. Good luck with that!

It was late Sunday afternoon, and Lynda was making a pot of spaghetti sauce and some spicy meatballs for dinner. She loved cooking on the weekends, when she had time to enjoy the process. She had opened a bottle of Malbec to enjoy while she was cooking. The sauce was simmering brightly on the stove and the kitchen was fragrant when Ben walked in.

He glanced at her briefly.

"Hi Mom," said Ben.

"Hi honey," said Lynda. "I'm making spaghetti and meatballs."

"Oh, good. That sounds great," he replied.

"Sweetie, come sit with me. I'd like to talk to you."

Ben rolled his eyes. He was not in the mood for a lecture. He really just wanted to get something to eat, take a shower, and hang out in his room; alone.

Lynda pulled a stool up to the kitchen island. She grabbed a can of sparkling juice out of the fridge and handed it to him.

"Come on, honey, I haven't seen you all weekend. I don't even know where you were last night. We need to talk for a few minutes," she said. "I'm not mad at you. I'm not going to lecture or yell at you. We just need to talk to each other."

Ben hesitated for a moment, then he took the juice and sat on the stool. The spaghetti and meatballs smelled so good. He supposed he could talk to her for just a little while. He sat down on the stool and opened his drink.

"Honey, I'm worried about you," said Lynda. "It's dangerous for you to be involved in drugs, and it's illegal. You need to stop."

"Mom, there is nothing wrong with pot. That's all I'm doing; not heroine, not coke, not pills. Just pot. It's ridiculous that it's illegal, and I know that's going to change soon," he argued.

"It may change," Lynda agreed. "But right now, at this time and in Texas, it's illegal."

"The cops are really lenient about pot. They really don't care if you have it."

Lynda grinned. "Where in the world did you hear that? I don't think that's true."

"Everybody knows that," said Ben. "The cops know that it's going to be legal soon, so they just don't care."

"Honey, that's not true. I spoke with an officer yesterday to find out what the laws are. They do care about marijuana users. It's illegal, and if you're caught breaking the law there will be consequences."

Ben was shocked. "You talked to the cops? Why?"

"Because I want to be informed," said Lynda. "I want to know exactly what the legal consequences are if you get caught."

"I'm not gonna get caught."

"You might get caught," said Lynda.

Ben was getting annoyed. "You know, as soon as I'm eighteen, I'm going to move back to Colorado where pot's legal," he said.

"When you're eighteen, you can do whatever you like," replied Lynda. "But you do understand that even in Colorado, you can't buy it unless you're twenty-one, right?"

"Why do you know these things?" asked Ben. "You don't smoke it; you're not interested."

"I watch the news, honey. There was a lot of information on TV when it was becoming legal in Colorado and Washington. It's regulated in a very similar way to alcohol. You have to be twenty-one. You can't even go into one of the dispensaries if you're underage."

"Okay, speaking of alcohol, you drink wine almost every night," said Ben.

Lynda was expecting this argument, and she was prepared.

"I'm old enough to walk into a store and buy a bottle of wine. It's perfectly legal. And, even if I have a couple of glasses of wine in the evening, I still get up at 5:30 almost every morning. I go to work, and do everything that I need to do."

"But alcohol causes a lot of deaths every year, and marijuana has never caused any," stated Ben. "You never see an 'angry stoned person' like you see an 'angry drunk.' It's much safer."

Lynda knew that her son would have an answer for every argument that she presented. That was okay; he was entitled to his own opinion. But that's all it was; an opinion. She didn't believe that he had any hard facts to support his argument.

As she spent the past couple of days performing research, she learned that there is a particular culture of individuals who believe that there is nothing wrong with smoking marijuana on a regular basis and living within a perpetual state of being high. These people believe that weed is a miracle drug. It does everything from helping you sleep well at night to curing chronic pain and even cancer.

During the time that Colorado and Washington were going through the process to legalize marijuana, Lynda had watched several documentaries on the medicinal properties of pot. She understood that patients who benefited from THC typically did not smoke it, and they didn't get high. THC extract is available in an oil form which can even be used by children.

She had seen the stories of five-year-old children who suffered from chronic seizures. Their parents and doctors had tried all possible medications, with little to no improvement. For some reason, the THC oil could help reduce the frequency of seizures by fifty percent.

So, yes, she understood that there were potential medical uses for marijuana, and that there needed to be further testing. Pot is far from the cure-all miracle drug that some people believed it to be. The theory that cannabis can cure cancer and Alzheimer's disease is a bit far-fetched.

There's a saying in the medical community about a "cure-all;" it cures nothing.

But helping with certain types of seizures, and helping to relieve a cancer patient's chronic pain? Lynda didn't have a problem with that at all. She didn't even have a problem with people using it for recreational purposes.

She expressed this opinion to Ben.

"As long as it's regulated, like alcohol is, I don't think it's a problem. Even when it is legalized in a state, someone your age cannot buy it or use it, right?"

Ben scowled. "It shouldn't be like that. I know what I can and can't handle. "

Lynda smiled. She remembered being a teenager, and

being sure that she knew more than her parents did, especially her mom.

"I know you do, honey, but you have to follow the law. The laws are there for a reason. If you think you can handle smoking pot at fifteen, you'll probably have a thirteen-year-old saying the same thing, then an eleven-year-old. Do you think it's okay for kids that young to make that decision?" she asked him.

"No, I guess not," he said, grumpily. Lynda felt that he might be starting to see her point of view.

"Honey, until you're out of the house and taking care of yourself, it's my job to make sure nothing happens to you. I have to help you make the right decisions. You're still learning."

Ben took a drink of his juice. He was starting to get tired of this conversation.

"And being stoned all the time isn't healthy. You understand that, don't you?" asked Lynda. "You'll lose motivation to do anything productive."

"Mom, I'm not stoned all the time," he replied. "I do have trouble sleeping, and smoking pot helps me get to sleep, and stay asleep."

"Ben, if you were more active during the day, you wouldn't have any trouble sleeping!" Lynda was rather surprised to hear this from her son. What fifteen-year-old had trouble sleeping? Teenagers often slept more than toddlers.

"You should get out and exercise!" she told him. "I bought that gym membership for you last year. Do you ever go?"

"No," mumbled Ben.

"That is something you can easily do to help with

sleeping. Exercising regularly also helps increase your energy level and helps you focus on your work."

"Mom, you sound like a commercial."

Lynda chuckled. "I suppose I do," she said. "I just feel very strongly that regular exercise is vital to physical and mental health. It's one of the most important things you can do for yourself."

"Yeah, I know you think that Mom," said Ben. "When's dinner going to be ready?"

"Soon, honey," said Lynda. "Look, I need to make sure you understand something. If you decide to defy the rules of this house and the state laws by using drugs, then I'm not going to help you. I'm not going to bail you out of jail. I'm not going to pay for legal fees. Your college fund will be used for that. Also, I'm not going to let you get a driver's license as long as you're doing this. I know that's something you're looking forward to. But you need to understand, that's a privilege. Driving is not a right."

Ben was not expecting to hear this. He knew that he would be eligible to start going to driving school within the next few months, and he had been counting on that.

"What about driving school?" he asked his mother. "I'm supposed to sign up for lessons soon."

"That's my point," replied Lynda. "If you make getting high a priority, I'm not paying for driving school, or doing anything to help you get a license. I'm not going to help put a stoner behind the wheel."

Lynda could see that Ben was becoming agitated.

"Mom, I'm not a stoner!" he was close to shouting. "I told you, pot is not dangerous, and it won't affect my driving!"

"Ben, calm down. I'm simply telling you what you can

expect if you continue this behavior. I'm not okay with it. You need to understand that. If you choose to keep going down this road, there will be consequences that you probably won't like."

Lynda was actually nervous as she explained these rules to her son. She didn't understand why! She's the parent; she's the one with the power to make and enforce the rules. So, why did she feel this way?

She supposed it had something to do with wanting her son to like her. In her heart, Lynda wanted to be best friends with her son. Her head told her otherwise. She knew that Ben had plenty of friends, and she didn't need to be one of them. That's actually one of the biggest mistakes a parent can make; she actually became pretty judgmental of other parents when she saw them try to be buddies with their children. Ben has plenty of friends, but only one mother. Lynda knew she needed to be strong.

The conversation with Officer Hughes helped boost her confidence. She had forgotten that she really had the power to lay down the law with her son. It didn't matter if he liked it or not.

Ben glared at her. He was speechless. He had been counting on getting his permit in a couple of months, and his driver's license six months later. And, he was hoping that his grandfather would contribute some money toward a used car fund, like he had for Ben's older brother.

"I'm getting my permit soon," he said to his mom.

"Not if you don't follow the house rules," replied Lynda. "Honey, honestly, they're not that bad. Don't drink or do drugs while you're underage. Get decent grades. Help out around the house when I need you. I'm really not that strict."

Ben did not agree with his mother. She might not think she was very strict but in his opinion, she was infringing upon his individual rights. He wholeheartedly believed that he could make the right decisions for himself. He did not need her micro-managing his life anymore.

But he didn't voice these opinions to his mother.

"Okay," he said. "Can I have some food?"

"Sure, sweetie, I'll fix a plate for you." Lynda smiled. She felt relieved. Sometimes, all it takes is a good heart-to-heart conversation. She just needed to lay everything out on the table for Ben to understand exactly what is expected from him, and what he could expect in return.

Monday Afternoon

Lynda stared across the large conference table at the product manager. His scalp was glistening beneath the harsh fluorescent lights, dimmed only by the strands of his come-over. She wasn't sure she had correctly heard what he had just told her.

"You need me to provide training to the Tech Support team when?" she asked.

"Tomorrow," he replied. "It's scheduled for three o'clock eastern."

He fiddled nervously with a pen. Lynda could tell that he knew how annoyed she was, but she doubted that he cared.

"Why am I just learning about this now?"

"Lynda," the product manager's boss was chiming in. "We know this is last minute. Unfortunately, training kind of fell between the cracks. Don just remembered that Tech Support scheduled this session for tomorrow. But you've already written the manual, right? Just do some cutting and pasting into PowerPoint, and it'll be fine."

"Who's giving the training?" Lynda asked, fearing that she already knew the answer.

"You're a great trainer!" grinned Don's boss. "And the Tech Support team already knows you. They feel comfortable with you."

"I think Don should be there too, in case there are any questions I can't answer," Lynda replied.

"Of course, he'll be right there with you," the boss said. "Thanks for your help, Lynda."

The three of them left the room, and walked off in three different directions.

Lynda was annoyed, but she realized that in the grand scheme of things, this wasn't too bad. She just hated having tasks sprung on her at the last freaking minute! With the proper notice, she could have created a really comprehensive and informative training session. Now, she'd be lucky to get the main points across to the Tech Support guys. She hated doing things half-assed.

Back at her desk, she looked at the time displayed on her iPhone. It was almost four; great. Looks like it would be a late night tonight. She sent Ben a quick text message, explaining that she needed to work late and that he could have leftover spaghetti for dinner.

Ben: Okay Mom.

Lynda: Feed Fritzi too!

Ben: I will.

That was taken care of. Lynda sat at her desk, and opened PowerPoint, to start the training presentation, and Word, which displayed the manual she had completed the previous week. Thank goodness she had the two monitors connected to her laptop. She didn't know how she'd be able to get her job done with just one screen. Don's boss had been somewhat correct in his assessment; she'd be doing a bit of copying and pasting in order to get the training material finished as quickly as possible.

Lynda plugged in her earbuds, and fired up a podcast

from the Maximum Fun website. There was a new Judge John Hodgman show that she hadn't listened to yet. That would make her task easier, and the time would go by more quickly.

She had completed twenty-six slides and was listening to the judge hear a case about a woman who thought her husband had way too many socks, when her phone rang. The number was local, but she didn't recognize it. She normally didn't answer calls from numbers she didn't know. They were usually from a telemarketer, or some kind of crazy scam. But the prefix looked like it could be close to home, so she decided to make an exception.

She glanced at the time displayed on her monitor; it was just after eight o'clock.

"Hello, this is Lynda," she said as she answered.

"Hi there, Ms. Murphy," said a man's voice. "This is Officer Roy Hughes with the Rosemeade Police Department."

Lynda perked up immediately. Officer Friendly was calling her! This could be very cool. Maybe he was calling to ask her out! She thought she had sensed a connection the other night at the police station.

"Oh, yes, hi! How are you?"

"Well, I'm fine, but I'm afraid that I have some bad news for you," he said.

This didn't sound like he was going to ask her out. "What is it?" she asked.

"About twenty minutes ago your son was brought in for possession of marijuana. He was with some friends, but we weren't able to apprehend them."

Lynda closed her eyes. She was devastated, yet not completely surprised. As she had told her son, if you participate in illegal activities, you'll eventually get caught. He hadn't believed her. He thought he was invincible. Most teenagers did.

As a mom, as a parent, what was Lynda's best course of action? Her first instinct was to jump up and go get her baby. But she forced herself to remain still and calm, and take a deep breath. She asked herself the question, "What is the best thing for my son?"

Lynda opened her eyes. She took a deep breath, then asked, "Officer Hughes, how long can I leave him there? With you? In jail?"

There was a pause before he answered.

"Well, you understand that because he's a minor, you're responsible for him, correct?"

"Yes, I understand," Lynda replied. "I'm hoping that if he stays in jail for a couple of days, it'll help wake him up."

He chuckled.

"I get that," he said. "And it wouldn't be the first time we've done something like that. We don't have a prison here, or an extended stay facility. We can't do much more than keep him for two nights."

"Okay," said Lynda. "If that's all right with you, I think that might help."

She hesitated before speaking again. What if Officer Hughes thought she was being a bad parent by leaving her son in jail? Did he understand that she was just trying to help him?

"I hope you don't think I'm just trying to pass the buck," she said to the officer. "I feel like I've been talking and talking to him until I'm blue in the face, and he won't listen. If I leave him in jail for a couple days, I'm hoping that might knock some sense into him."

"Oh, I understand completely," he replied. "Teenagers are not easy to convince. We can give this a try. He'll have three hots and a cot."

Lynda smiled. "Three hots and a cot" was a funny term.

"But," Officer Hughes continued, "This won't be the end for him. Your son, and you, will need to appear before a judge and there will be a sentence. Since this is his first offense it probably won't be more than community service, but you both need to be there."

"I understand," she said. "I just think that if he is forced to stay in jail for a couple of days it would mean more than if I ran over and got him out."

"Yes, I agree," said Officer Hughes. "I'm happy to help. You can come by any time you like to see him. We'll keep him in a holding cell. Just check in with the officer at the front desk, and he'll help you. Today's Monday; let's plan on you coming to pick him up on Wednesday. Will that work?"

"Sure, that's very helpful. Can I come by after work?" she asked.

"Yeah, that'll be fine."

"Okay. If there's anything you need from me in the meantime, please let me know."

"I'll do that," said Officer Hughes. "You have a good night."

Lynda hung up the phone. She took several deep breaths to calm herself. Her son was in jail. At least she knew where he was, and that he was safe. When life gives her lemons, she tries to find the lemonade.

She was close to being finished with the training presentation and decided that it was time to be finished for the night. The words on the screen were starting to swim in front of her eyes. Lynda was done. Someone needed to stick a fork in her.

She locked her computer for the night, and packed up to go home.

The training session went very well, even though Don didn't do much to contribute. He spent most of the time messing with his phone. By the time they were finished it was a little after five, so Lynda started getting ready to leave the office.

Lynda hadn't talked to Ben at all during the past twenty-four hours, but she was planning to stop by the police station on her way home from work. She had packed a small bag for him that morning; a change of underwear, a toothbrush, and his glasses.

She walked through the main doors of the police station, carrying the light blue drawstring bag containing the toiletry items.

"Hello," she greeted the officer behind the desk. It wasn't Officer Hughes this evening.

"My son is Ben Murphy, and he's staying here for a few days," she said. "I've brought him a few things."

"Oh, sure, Roy told me all about this project," replied the officer. "Trying a little 'scared straight' on your son, right? Let's see what's in the bag, please."

"Well, I'm hoping it might work," she said, as she placed the bag on the desk.

"It's certainly worth a try," he said, as he quickly checked Ben's belongings, then handed the bag back to Lynda. "Looks like you didn't bring a cake with a file in it, so you're good to go. I'll walk you back to the holding area."

"Thank you," she said.

Lynda followed the officer through a large set of double doors, after he unlocked them using a security card. They traveled down a short hallway that contained two desks, neither of which were occupied, then went through another set of locked doors.

That's where she saw her son.

Ben was in the first of four cells that made up a large room. He had been lying on the bunk with his hands clasped behind his head, and he jumped up swiftly when he heard the approaching footsteps.

"Mom!" he exclaimed when he saw Lynda.

"Hi Ben," she replied.

"Ma'am, I'll be right outside this door," said the officer. "Just knock when you're ready to leave."

Lynda smiled at him and nodded. Then she turned back to her son.

"I brought you some things I thought you might need," she said as she held the bag toward him.

He didn't take it. His eyes were wide with shock.

"What are you talking about? Aren't you here to take me home?"

"No, I'm not," she replied. "I think it's a good idea for you to stay here for one more night to think about your behavior and the consequences."

Ben stared at his mother. His cheeks were flushed with anger; even his ears were bright red. He grabbed his hair with both hands in what looked like an effort to retain some control. It wasn't working very well.

"That is bullshit!" he yelled at the top of his voice, and slammed the bars of the cell with his hands.

"What the hell is wrong with you? You can't just leave me here! It was only a little weed! I didn't do anything wrong!"

Lynda was shocked. She just stood there and stared at her son. She was fighting to stay calm and not return his fire.

"You broke the law. This is what we discussed the other day. If you break the law, there are consequences."

"Fine, but you're supposed to get me out of here and take me home! You're my mom, that's your freaking job!" he shouted at her.

"Really? I've never seen that written anywhere. I'm not your personal get-out-of-jail-free card."

Lynda tossed the drawstring bag between the bars, where it landed on the cell floor.

"You have tonight and tomorrow to think about what you've done, and come up with an attitude adjustment plan," she told him. She paused for a moment and looked into his wild eyes once more. Then she turned and knocked on the door to summon the officer who would lead her out of the station.

Tuesday Afternoon

Matt was in the high school locker room, getting ready to suit up for football practice. Just like any other town in Texas, Rosemeade was crazy for football. This was Matt's first year as a starter for the team, and he was ready for the Friday night lights to start shining again.

The guys were horsing around and smack-talking, taking off their street clothes and putting on their uniforms. Matt looked around and saw that most of the team was there, and everyone was in a great mood. They were all ready for a great season.

"Good afternoon, gentlemen!" the coach boomed as he entered the locker room. "We're going to start the day with a surprise drug test. Get ready to pee in a cup!"

Matt froze. He had forgotten about random drug tests. There had been one around the beginning of the previous season, but that was before he had started hanging around with Ben and getting high. He had nothing to worry about at that time. Now he did.

"We're testing you for marijuana today. You all understand that it's not possible to use marijuana in any form and play football for this team. This is not news to any of you. You know the drill; if you think you're going to fail the test, you can leave now. You're off the team.

Otherwise, take a cup." He began handing plastic cups to each player.

Coach reached the player standing next to Matt and held out a cup. The boy didn't take it. He stood with his hands in his pockets, staring at his feet.

"Stevens, are you refusing to take this test?" Coach asked.

Stevens didn't look up.

"Yes sir," he said.

"Well, that sucks. Take off your uniform, and leave it on the bench."

Matt didn't know what to do. Stevens was humiliated and Matt did not want to go through that. Having to admit that in front of the coach and the entire team, and then take off his uniform would be unbearable.

When Coach handed the cup to Matt, he took it. He knew he wouldn't pass the test, but he could not go through the public embarrassment of admitting it in front of the entire team. After Coach had distributed all the cups, Stevens had been the only one who had refused the test.

The boys wrote their names on their assigned cups with a Sharpie, and filed into the restroom to make their deposits.

Matt was terrified. He thought about diluting his urine with water, but he didn't really think it would help. That would probably just reduce the THC concentration, but he knew it would still be detected. It was only a couple of nights ago that he and Ben had last smoked.

He looked around the restroom, to see which of his teammates were with him. Would any of them be willing to give him some of their urine? How would he even ask them for something like that?

"Hey, dude, can I have some of your piss?" He couldn't imagine uttering those words.

The restroom door opened, and one more person entered; the assistant coach.

"Okay gentlemen, do what you need to do so we can get out of here," he said. Apparently he had been sent in as a lookout.

"Crap," thought Matt. There was absolutely nothing he could do, except pee in the cup; and get kicked off the team.

As each player completed their task, they placed the cup on a table in the equipment room. Its surface had been cleared specifically for this purpose. Coach led the players out to the field to begin practice, while the assistant coach stayed behind to conduct the tests. Matt looked at the table as he passed by; a stack of testing sticks lay in the middle, just waiting to be dipped in Matt's cup of pee, and end his football career.

The team was running their second lap around the field when the assistant coach appeared and said something to Coach. Matt was too far away to see Coach's face, but he could imagine the expression; it would certainly be a combination of anger, disgust, and disappointment.

Coach pointed to Matt. "Martinez, come see me," he said, and turned to go back into the locker rooms.

Finally, Coach turned around to look at Matt squarely in the eye.

"Son, what the hell is wrong with you?" he asked. Matt couldn't look at him. He dropped his eyes to the floor.

"Look me in the eye!" Coach commanded. Matt obeyed.

"We've known each other for a while now, and I have

never known you to be so careless. When Stevens took off his gear and left, I honestly wasn't very surprised. He didn't really have the drive and the determination that serious players demonstrate. But you! You have promise! You have so much potential! And I've always been very clear about the consequences of using drugs on this team. You knew exactly what would happen."

Matt felt tears welling in his eyes.

Coach's tone softened. "Matt, you're a good kid. Why would you sacrifice everything just to smoke pot?"

Matt's voice caught as he answered, "I don't know, Coach. I'll never do it again, I promise."

"Matt, I can't let this go, you know that. As much as I want to, I can't let you slide and give you a second chance. You're off the team, son. Take off your gear, and leave it on the bench. Then you can go."

Coach paused, then he told Matt, "I need to send a letter to your folks. They will find out about this; there's no way around it. I think it would be better if they heard about it from you, instead of me."

Matt nodded. When the assistant coach had come into the restroom to monitor the football players, Matt fully realized the gravity of his situation. He realized that everything that was happening were the consequences of his own stupid actions. There was no one to blame but himself.

Coach left the locker room and let Matt gather his things, and his emotions, and leave.

Dottie was in the kitchen when Matt walked in through the door that leads to the garage. She didn't notice him enter; probably because it wasn't the right time, and the last thing she expected was for Matt to come home.

Her back was to him as he approached her. He thought about just going to his room, and dealing with the whole ugly mess later. But he realized that would just make it worse for him. The worrying and stewing would be worse than coming clean with his mom. Better to just rip the bandage off and get it over with.

"Hi Mom," he said. She jumped and quickly turned around to see what had startled her. Dottie always startled easily. There were times when Matt would just walk into the room where she was folding laundry, and she would let out a little shriek.

"Honey, what are you doing home so early?" she rushed to him, and placed her hand on his forehead and his cheeks.

"Are you sick?" she asked. "Did something happen at practice?" Matt knew that by "something" she didn't have the faintest idea that her golden son had been kicked off the team for failing a drug test. In her mind, the "something" would have been the coach getting sick, or the stadium burning down.

"Yeah, Mom, something happened," he said. "Can we talk?"

"Sure, sweetie," she answered in a very worried voice. "Let's sit down."

They went into the family room and sat next to each other on the couch.

Matt had tried to practice this conversation with his mother all the way home. He knew there was no way to sugar coat it. There was no way to keep her from being horribly disappointed in him, and absolutely devastated.

He took a deep breath, and just said it.

"There was a random drug test at practice today. I failed it. I'm off the team."

Dottie blinked. She didn't seem to understand. Matt was silent, giving her time to absorb what he had said.

"You're kidding. This is some kind of weird joke," she said. "It isn't funny."

"No," he replied, his voice almost a whisper. "It's not a joke."

"I don't understand, Matt. You don't do drugs." And then Dottie remembered the conversation that she had with Lynda Murphy several days earlier.

"Oh, my God. Have you been smoking pot with Ben Murphy? Is that what this is about?" she asked.

"Yes," replied Matt.

"Ben's mother called me the other day and told me this was happening, and I didn't believe her. I told her that my son would never do anything like that. My son knows that if he were caught doing drugs, he'd be kicked off the football team, and all chances for a scholarship would be gone."

Dottie was becoming agitated. Matt just sat there and kept quiet. There was nothing else he could do.

"You know that we have no money to pay for your college. We were all counting on you earning a scholarship, and you were on track to do that! Not to mention that you've been breaking the law!"

"I know."

"You know?" exclaimed Dottie. "You know?" She was becoming even more upset, and her voice was just short of yelling.

"Apparently you didn't know, because you have seriously screwed up!"

She stood up abruptly and turned her back to her son. One hand was on her hip, and she held the other to her face. Matt was pretty sure she was crying. He felt lower than low. Lower than a worm. The worst thing he could do was make his mother cry. He felt his own throat tighten.

"Mom, I'm so sorry," he said.

She whirled around to face him; the tears were streaming down her face. Matt couldn't remember ever seeing her like this. She jabbed her right index finger in the air toward him.

"Do you know what the worst part of this is?" she demanded. "The worst part is that I defended you when Lynda Murphy called me and said she thought you and Ben were getting high together. I told her it was impossible. I said that you would never use drugs because you understood what was important and you would never jeopardize that!"

That sent Matt over the edge; he started crying, too.

"Mommy, I'm so sorry," he choked out.

Dottie took a deep breath, in an effort to control herself.

"I can't look at you right now. Go to your room," she said.

Matt left that room as fast as he possibly could, sat on his bed, and sobbed.

Dottie considered calling her husband at work to give him the whole scoop, but she thought it would be best if she calmed down first. She returned to the kitchen where she finished dinner. Ralph would be home soon enough, anyway. She grabbed a glass beer mug out of the cupboard, and put it in the freezer. When he walked in the door, the plan was to make sure he was as happy as possible before she told him the day's story. A frosty mug of beer after work would certainly help his mood.

Ralph walked in the front door promptly as six o'clock. He was so predictable! Dottie loved that about him. She was all about stability in her family and her home. If he was going to be late, he would call. It had been that way for the nineteen years of their marriage, and she didn't expect anything to change.

She presented her husband with a chilly Shiner bock, poured expertly into the frosty mug. The beer had about half an inch of foam on it, just like he liked it. Not too much, not too little.

A wide grin spread across Ralph's face.

"Wow, thanks, honey!" he exclaimed as he set down his briefcase and car keys. "I must have done something right today and I didn't even know it!"

But the look in her eyes made him reconsider that statement.

"Or you have something to tell me, and you're trying to butter me up before you do."

Ralph took a deep swallow of the dark beer.

"Okay, I'm ready," he declared. "Hit me."

Dottie opened a Shiner for herself before answering her husband. They both stood in the kitchen as she recounted the entire story, including the part about the phone call from Lynda Murphy. She felt especially bad about that.

When she finished, Ralph was quiet. He was thinking about how to respond to his wife, Dottie could see that. She thought he must be furious; he was hiding it well, keeping a lid on his anger. Finally, he started to speak.

"Honey," he began, "You and I met when we were

seniors in college, right?"

Dottie nodded. Of course; who wouldn't remember how they met their spouse? It was a crazy situation; they had both been in Freshman Composition together. They were seniors, taking Freshman Comp! This class is normally a prerequisite for all freshmen. They can't take any other English classes without either attending or testing out of Freshman Comp. For both Ralph and Dottie, this class had somehow slipped through the cracks for both of them. There was no way around graduating without earning these three credits.

Dottie didn't mind so much because she was a Liberal Arts major. It was kind of a blow-off class for her. Nice and easy at the end of her college career.

Ralph, on the other hand, was not pleased. He was an Electrical Engineering major who had no use for a composition class. He was busy learning about wave theory; he didn't give a crap about subjects, verbs, and objects.

As the only two seniors in the class, Ralph and Dottie gravitated toward each other. They soon learned of each other's situations, and the cute, petite brunette was happy to help this dark, hunky guy with his compositions. They married six months after graduation.

Now, Ralph studied the beer in his mug as he collected his thoughts.

"You didn't know me when I was in high school. I had a bit of a wild streak," he said.

"But weren't you the captain of the baseball team?" she asked him.

"Yes, that's true, I was. And I was still kind of wild." He paused for a moment before he said, "I did my share of partying. I think everyone does at that age. Kids are experimenting and testing their limits. I don't think it's the end of the world."

"Ralph, he was kicked off the team! We've been counting on Matt getting a football scholarship so he can go to college! I don't know how we're going to make that happen now."

Ralph reached for Dottie's hand.

"We'll make it work. We'll find a way," he said. "A lot of kids today go to community college for the first two years, then finish at a university. That's something we can easily pay for, and he can just live at home. We'll make it work."

Dottie sighed. "Okay," she said. "I'm just so disappointed and hurt. I can't believe he's been doing this behind our backs."

Ralph chuckled. "Yeah, that's usually how it works. Not many kids will openly tell their parents they're getting high. Did he at least seem like he was sorry? Or did he act like it isn't a big deal?"

"Oh, he's definitely sorry," said Dottie. "He said so, many times. And he was crying."

"I think that's a good sign. If he didn't feel any remorse, then I'd be worried. He knows he did something wrong. He probably won't do this again."

"You're probably right," she said. "What really gets me is that he just threw away his future! It's gone!"

"No, honey, it's not," replied Ralph. "He made a mistake. Yes, it was definitely a big one, but his life isn't over. It'll just take a different direction now. I'm sure that he learned from it."

Dottie wasn't completely convinced. "We'll see," she

said. "Hey, you're going to have to act like you're a little angry about this when you see him. You're much too calm right now."

"Don't worry," said Ralph. "I'll put my mad face on." His mouth turned downward into a frown and he partially closed his eyes, until they were almost slits. Ralph crossed his arms against his chest and said, in a low voice, "How's this?"

Dottie giggled. "That's pretty good," she said. "I'd be afraid of you if I didn't know you so well. Let's go finish getting dinner ready."

They got up to make their way toward the kitchen.

"I think after dinner I need to call Lynda and apologize," said Dottie.

"Yeah, that's a good idea," said Ralph. "She could probably use a friend."

Dottie nodded. She would be sure to call Lynda after dinner. She felt so bad for not believing her. There had really been no cause to completely dismiss Lynda's suspicions. Lynda hadn't been rude when she had called Dottie. Dottie realized now that she was simply concerned, and trying to discover the truth. But Dottie had refused to believe that her baby boy could possibly do anything wrong.

She felt like an idiot. Ralph was right, of course. Teenagers do things they're not supposed to. They're testing their independence. They've been doing this since the beginning of time. And it's her job as a parent to correct any behavior that isn't acceptable.

Ralph was holding a beefsteak tomato and a bunch of basil.

"Caprese salad, right?" he asked.

"Sure, honey, that sounds good," replied Dottie. She reached into the pantry for the olive oil and balsamic vinegar.

"You know," she said thoughtfully, "There's going to have to be some kind of punishment, or consequences for Matt. We can't just let this go."

"I was thinking that, too," said Ralph. "Although, being booted from the team is a pretty decent consequence. He won't be able to play any other team sports, either."

"That's true," mused Dottie. "You know, I had always thought that having him in sports all these years would keep him out of trouble."

"I know, right? A guy at work told me a story once about his daughter getting caught at an all-night booze party. She was a straight-A, honor roll student. This was the last thing he had expected from her. Know what he told me?"

Dottie shook her head.

"He said that there are no good kids. I know that's an exaggeration, but his point was that all kids try to get away with things they know they're not supposed to do."

"But that doesn't make it okay!" Dottie exclaimed. "We can't just turn our heads and act like we don't care what he does!"

"And we won't, honey, don't worry," Ralph assured her.

"He should get a job," grumbled Dottie.

"That is an excellent idea! Somewhere that conducts random drug testing." Ralph was grinning; that would be a great way to teach Matt how to be responsible.

"Okay, I'll go out with him tomorrow after school, and we can apply at different places," said Dottie. She really liked this idea, too. But she didn't think it was enough.

There needed to be consequences; some kind of punishment.

"How about," she began, "if we take his iPhone for a while, and all access to his electronics?"

"He would certainly feel some pain," replied Ralph. "How about homework? I know he needs a computer to do his schoolwork."

"He can use a laptop here in the kitchen with me, and I can check on him," said Dottie. "Would that work?"

"Sure, that sounds like a great plan."

"Okay, good, it's a plan." Dottie was feeling better; she felt that they had a definite course of action for dealing with Matt's behavior. They weren't angry, and they weren't going to yell or scream at Matt. They were simply enforcing consequences that were the natural result of unacceptable behavior. It was a no-brainer.

"I'll get Matt to set the table," she said to Ralph, "and then we can eat." She smiled at her husband as the left the kitchen.

Tuesday Evening

It was almost seven-thirty that Tuesday evening when Dottie pulled up in front of Lynda's house. Autumn was approaching quickly, and the days were becoming noticeably shorter. The sun had almost set; she could see that lights were on in Lynda's house. She killed the motor and grabbed the grocery bag that was resting on the passenger seat.

Lynda was just finishing a quick dinner when the doorbell rang. She had been perusing many websites that discussed the issue of drug use, especially marijuana, among high school students.

She stopped what she was doing, feeling annoyed. She really didn't want to be bothered; it was probably some college kids selling knives door-to-door. Maybe she should just ignore them, and not answer. The bell rang a second time. Crap. She got up to answer it.

"Hi Lynda."

Lynda was stunned; Dottie Martinez stood on her front porch holding a Trader Joe's shopping bag.

"Hi Dottie," said Lynda. "What can I do for you?"

"Can I come in please? I really need to talk to you," replied Dottie.

Lynda held the door open and Dottie entered. They

both walked into the kitchen where Dottie place the Trader Joe's bag on the island.

"I'm here to apologize," began Dottie. She could tell by the puzzled expression on Lynda's face that she didn't understand. "For being so rude to you when you called, and not believing you."

"Oh," Lynda was beginning to understand. Something had happened with Matt. "What happened, Dottie?"

"I'll tell you in a minute, but first, I have a peace offering for you." Dottie reached into the bag and pulled out a bottle of Cabernet and a huge bar of dark chocolate.

Lynda started to laugh.

"Oh my gosh! How did you know how much I love this chocolate?" she picked up the Trader Joe's Pound Plus bar. "Thank you, Dottie, this is so nice of you."

"Honey, I just feel so bad for not believing a word you said. I was all about how perfect my boy was, and how there was no way in the world he'd ever start doing drugs. Can you forgive me?"

"Hey, you brought me wine and chocolate! Of course I forgive you!" Lynda looked at her friend. Her eyes were worried; she looked like she was truly worried that Lynda wouldn't forgive her.

"Dottie, you're my friend. I'm so glad you're here. Of course I forgive you. I didn't want to believe it either, when I first found out what Ben was doing. But then I realized that I had to believe it, and I had to do something about it." Lynda pulled one of the kitchen stools up to the island and opened the bar of rich, dark chocolate. She broke off pieces for both of them.

"Tell me your story," said Lynda. "What happened with Matt?"

Dottie explained everything that had happened that day. Lynda made sure she just let her friend speak, without interruption. When she had finished, Lynda said, "I think the fact that he's feeling remorseful is a very good sign. He understands that what he did was wrong. Ben didn't show any of that."

"Where is Ben now?" Dottie asked. "I was expecting to see him."

"He's in jail," Lynda replied casually.

"What?" Dottie was shocked! In jail? When had this happened? "I think it's your turn to tell me a story now!"

Lynda recounted the events of the past several days.

"Okay," said Dottie. "I think the big question is, 'What do we do?' There must be something that we can to do try to put a stop to this. Where are the boys getting the pot?"

"I'm not sure," replied Lynda. "I suppose there could be dealers here in town; or maybe kids are getting it in Dallas and bringing it here to sell."

Lynda thought for a moment.

"Let me get the iPod that I found in Ben's room. There might be some information that I missed before," she said.

"Oh, and I have Matt's phone!" Dottie exclaimed. She had made her son give up his phone after dinner. She and Ralph had explained, in a very calm manner, that an expensive smart phone is a privilege that he didn't deserve at the moment. He didn't argue, and handed it to him mom.

Lynda returned a minute later with Ben's iPod.

"Does Matt have the Twitter app on his phone?" she asked. "That's where I saw most of the messages. They use the direct messaging part of Twitter to talk to each other."

Dottie was scrolling through the phone's menu. "Yes,

here it is," she said.

She tapped the little blue bird icon, and launched the app. Lynda did the same on Ben's iPod.

"Wow……look at all of this!" Dottie was scrolling through the Twitter messages on her son's phone, discovering all of the pot related items that Lynda had discovered several days earlier on the iPod.

"I know," said Lynda grimly. "I was shocked at how far back the messages went. It sounds like they're getting most of the pot from SupaFreek. They were talking about meeting at school and making an exchange there."

"Do you know who that is?" Dottie asked.

"No, but there might be a way we can find out," said Lynda.

She walked to the family room, picked up her laptop, and brought it to the kitchen island. She pointed her browser to Twitter.com and logged in.

"If SupaFreek's Twitter profile isn't private, we might be able to get some information from it," she said.

Lynda entered SupaFreek in the search field at the top of the screen. Many results were returned; most of them messages, and tweets. She scrolled down a bit more, and found a heading marked "Accounts." There, she found what she was looking for. She clicked the SupaFreek account, and gazed into the face of David Wright. She knew this kid. She had given him a ride several times when he and Ben had gone to the movies, or to the mall. Lynda had always thought he was one of the good ones.

Dottie was peering over her shoulder at the computer screen.

"Do you know him?" she asked.

"Yes," Lynda replied. "That's David Wright. He lives

with his grandparents; I don't know where his parents are. They live over by Ellis Elementary."

"Geez, look at those pictures! And those messages!" Dottie was shocked; all over David Wright's Twitter page were pictures of pot, of people smoking pot, and messages about how great it was to be high.

The banner photo was an image of David smoking from a bong. His head was bent over the bong, and it looked like he was inhaling deeply. His shaggy blond hair hid his eyes. The profile photo showed the young man holding an unlit joint playfully between his thumb and index finger, with a wide grin on his face.

"I guess he doesn't realize that anyone can see these pictures," Lynda said. "Or maybe he just doesn't care."

She scrolled down the page.

"Look at this message. It says, 'Need some? I got it!' He's advertising his pot business right here! How is that legal?" Lynda asked.

"I have no idea," replied Dottie. "Should we call his grandparents, like you called me?"

"Sure," Lynda moved her eyes from the screen, to look at her friend. "Let's check the Internet and see what we can find."

Lynda entered several combinations of words into the Google search field. She tried, "David Wright," "Wright Rosemeade High School," and "Wright Rosemeade." She finally got lucky with the last one. A result was displayed on a city address website..

"This shows an address, but no phone number," Lynda told Dottie.

"Oh, you have an address?" Dottie was excited; that was progress! "Let's go over there and talk to them! You can bring Ben's iPod, and I have Matt's phone. We'll show them the evidence; they'll have to do something."

"Okay, sure, we can do that! You're right, they'll have to listen to us, and do something about the problem. Do you want to drive?" Lynda grabbed the iPod and her purse, and gave Fritzi a quick pat as the two women went on their mission.

David Wright's home was a short, ten minute drive from Lynda's, in one of the newer housing developments. Dottie parked the car in front of two story house. It was nice! The sun had set completely, and the house was illuminated by dramatic spotlights. The stone facade and three car garage were washed in bright light.

Lynda opened the passenger door, and looked at Dottie. "Are you ready?" she asked.

"You bet!" Dottie was still excited, and expecting a positive result. She was sure these people would get their grandson in line. The moms had proof; it was all over the Twitter.

The two women marched up the long, curving sidewalk like women on a mission, each carrying the proof of wrongdoing in their hands. Lynda rang the doorbell.

They heard a dog bark behind the door, and someone telling it to quiet down. A moment later the large, heavy-looking door was opened by a man who looked to be in his sixties. The thick shock of hair on his head was very white. He wore glasses with thick, dark frames.

He looked down at Dottie and Lynda; the combination of being about six feet, two inches tall, and standing on a step made him appear to be towering above them. He adjusted his glasses, as if to be able to see them better.

"Hello Mr. Wright," Lynda began. She hadn't met him

before, but she assumed that's who he was. When he didn't object, she realized that she had guessed correctly.

"We both have sons that go to school with your grandson, David," she continued. "We have reason to believe that David has been selling marijuana to our boys, and probably others."

He hesitated only for a moment before he spoke. His voice was deep. He talked to the two women as if he was used to being right, and getting his way.

"No, I'm sure you are mistaken. My grandson has nothing to do with drugs. I'd appreciate it if you get off my property. Good evening." He began closing the front door.

"But, Mr. Wright, we have proof on our cell phones!" Dottie practically shoved the phone under the man's nose, trying to force him to look at it. "There are many messages that show that your grandson has been bringing pot to school and selling it."

"Ladies!" his voice boomed. Lynda and Dottie were so stunned, they immediately became quiet and took a step back. "If you believe your sons are involved in some kind of illegal activity, then that's your problem. I am absolutely certain that my grandson is not involved. You need to leave now. Good-bye." And he slammed the large door.

For a long moment, there was complete silence on the empty street. Finally, Dottie said, "I guess we better go."

Lynda stood, staring at the large second story windows.

"I know he's up there," she said. "And I know he's the dealer."

"What can we do?" Dottie asked.

"Let's go to the police station. They were very helpful last time."

Rosemeade is a typical suburban town, and nothing is very far away. They arrived at the police station fifteen minutes later. Lynda was pleased to see Officer Hughes at the front desk. She knew that he would be helpful.

"Hi ladies," he greeted them warmly. "Are you here for Ben? I thought he was going home tomorrow, but I can go get him."

"Hi Officer Hughes," Lynda replied. "No, actually, I would like to wait until tomorrow. We're here for a different reason. We're pretty sure we found the boy who's selling pot to other kids."

She showed the officer the messages on the iPod, and also on Matt's phone.

"We just came from his house, and tried to talk to his grandfather," she explained. "He refused to believe his grandson was involved, and he threw us out. Is there anything you can do?"

"I can give the information to our narcotics team," said Officer Hughes. "I can't make any promises, but I'm happy to pass it along."

"That's it?" said Dottie. "We're absolutely sure that kid is selling pot! He's even bringing it to school!"

"It really is the only thing we can do right now," he replied gently. "I'm afraid I can't send a SWAT team to his home. You might want to call the high school tomorrow, and tell the crisis counselor."

"Sure, we can do that," said Lynda. "Come on, Dottie. We should go." The women walked quickly out of the police station.

"What's wrong?" asked Dottie. "Are you really letting it go, just like that?" She couldn't imagine Lynda just giving up. She had expected more assertiveness from her friend.

As they climbed back into the car Lynda said, "No, I'm not giving up. I get that the police need to handle this in their own way. And he had a good idea about calling the crisis counselor tomorrow. I know her. But, I have another idea, too." She smiled at Dottie.

"I don't know if I like the sound of this," murmured Dottie, as they drove out of the parking lot.

Thirty minutes later, after a quick stop at Kroger, the moms were back at the home of David Wright and his grandparents. This time, Lynda parked a few houses down the street from the Wright residence.

It was close to ten p.m.

"Ready?" Lynda asked Dottie.

"No, I'm not ready!" Dottie protested. "I think you're nuts! We're going to get caught!"

"No, we're not. It's totally dark out. Look, there are hardly any lights on this street. Kids get away with this all the time. We'll just be quiet, and it'll be fine." She opened the car door. "Let's go!"

Lynda took the lead, and Dottie reluctantly followed her. Their arms were full of white bundles.

Lynda stopped in front of the Wright house, right next to a large Bradford pear tree. The Bradford pear is a favorite of suburban Texas neighborhoods. It grows quickly, and produces beautiful small, white flowers in the spring.

It was very dark; luckily the porch light was off and not illuminating the yard. Only the spotlights lit the house. She grabbed a roll of toilet paper and hurled it high up into the branches of the tall tree. The roll unfurled as it rose, leaving a trail of white behind it. The roll got stuck in one of the branches. That was okay. They had plenty.

Dottie followed suit and tossed a roll of her own, but not quite as high as the one Lynda had thrown. That one looped a trail of TP over a branch, and landed on the ground. Dottie picked it up, and threw it again. If she hadn't been so paranoid about getting caught, and probably being arrested, she would have been having fun!

Lynda drew her arm back and chucked a roll as hard as she could. It went even higher into the branches before becoming lodged.

Dottie couldn't contain herself. "That was a good one!" she exclaimed.

"Shhhhhh! Not so loud!" said Lynda. But she was giggling also, trying too hard to remain silent.

Suddenly, the porch light turned on, and the front yard was flooded with light.

"Who's out there?" boomed a very loud, angry voice.

"Run!" Lynda said in a loud whisper. The two women sprinted down the sidewalk, back to the car. Lynda jumped in the driver's side and started the ignition. Dottie was barely in the passenger seat before Lynda stomped on the accelerator and zoomed down the street, out of the neighborhood.

The Bradford pear tree in the middle of the Wright's front yard was decorated with long, white streamers of toilet paper, waving in the slight breeze.

Wednesday Morning

Lynda didn't need her alarm to wake her the next morning. She had barely slept that night. Today is the day she would go to the police station and bring Ben home. Dottie had been great; after TP-ing the Wright's house, she hung out with Lynda at her house for a while. They cracked the bottle of wine that Dottie had brought, and talked about the boys.

The two women sat at the kitchen island with their wine glasses, trying to figure out their teenage sons.

"I don't think they're bad," said Lynda. "All teenagers experiment and get in trouble, right?"

"I think that's true," replied Dottie.

"Sure it is. What worries me is that when I caught Ben, he didn't show any remorse. He wasn't sorry. He acted like it was my fault for not letting him do what he wanted to."

"I know," said Dottie. She could tell that Lynda just needed to talk about what had happened, and about what she was feeling. Dottie knew she was lucky; she had Ralph. He was her best friend, and she could talk to him about absolutely everything. He didn't judge; he just listened. Even when she was acting crazy, and she totally knew she could be certifiably nuts sometimes, he was there for her. Lynda didn't have that.

"In the few days since I found out about all this," Lynda continued, "it seems like all he cares about is scoring his next high. All of the messages I've seen, and the things he's said to me; it's like he doesn't care about school, or about being successful in any way."

She covered her face with her hands. Lynda was so embarrassed; she was about to start crying, and she didn't think she could stop it.

"He doesn't give a shit about me, or our home, or the life that I'm trying to provide for the two of us!" She was openly crying now; tears were streaming down her face. "I don't know what I did wrong. I don't know why he's doing this."

"Oh, honey," Dottie put her arms around her friend. "I don't think you've done anything wrong. You can't blame yourself for this. Parents have been fighting with their teenagers for centuries!"

She grabbed a handful of tissues and gave them to Lynda. Lynda tried to wipe the tears from her face, but they kept coming. She blew her nose loudly.

"Dottie, it's been just him and me for so long. Tim has been out of the house for years, and it's just been Ben and me. I thought we had a good relationship! I just don't understand how he can behave like this!"

Fresh tears started; Dottie grabbed more tissues. Luckily, there was a full box on the island.

"You're picking him up from the police station tomorrow, right?" Lynda nodded her head.

"I'm dreading it," she said.

"Would you like me to come with you?" asked Dottie.

Lynda thought about that. She had actually been hoping that Dottie would offer. But even if she came to the police station with her, it was just delaying the inevitable. It was delaying the attitude she'd most likely have to deal with, and maybe even the fight they would have. Lynda thought it would be better to be strong, and pick him up herself.

She smiled at Dottie. "I really appreciate the offer, but I think it's something I need to do on my own."

"Okay," said Dottie. "I understand. But call me if I can do anything, all right? Anything at all."

So, after a good cry with a good friend, and a fairly sleepless night, she got herself caffeinated and showered, and on her way to work. As Lynda was walking toward the front door Fritzi walked directly in her path. That was odd; she never did that. The puppy was usually relaxing on her bed with a full belly by the time Lynda was ready to leave the house.

But this morning, she stood in front of Lynda and gave her a little nudge with her nose. Lynda knelt down, and wrapped her arms around her best friend. Dogs always knew, didn't they? They knew when their people were going on vacation, or moving, or when they were hurting. Fritzi knew that Lynda needed comfort, which is why she caught her before she left the house.

Lynda thought of an Internet meme she had seen recently. It said something like, "If you have a teenager in the house, make sure you have a dog. At least someone will be glad to see you when you get home." That one hit home.

She got through her work day easily enough. At least there weren't any meetings she had to sit through, or training sessions she needed to conduct.

Lynda did make two phone calls that day. The first was to Jennifer Griffin, the crisis counselor at the high school.

She filled her in with the events of the past few days, and also that she suspected that David Wright was the dealer.

"Lynda, that doesn't surprise me. His name has come up several times before regarding selling pot."

"Really?" Lynda was surprised. If that were the case, she would have thought his grandparents would have been more cooperative. "Have you talked to his grandparents?"

"Oh, yes," said Jennifer. "They're in complete denial. They won't discuss it. But there are some things I can do. Can you send me screenshots of the messages you have?"

"Of course," replied Lynda. "I'll e-mail them to you."

"Great. I'll take care of it. Don't worry."

"Thanks, Jennifer, I really appreciate your help. Let me know if there's anything else I can do."

The second call she made was to the police station, to coordinate a time to pick up Ben. Lynda and the officer agreed on 5:00, so she would need to leave work a little early. That wasn't a problem.

Lynda drove up in front of the station right on time. She hadn't talked to Ben since the other night, when he demanded he take her home. He had been in the holding cell for three days. Lynda really hoped that this time had given him the opportunity to think about the consequences he could face if he continued using drugs.

Officer Hughes was at the front desk.

"Hi Lynda," he greeted her. "Are you ready to take your son home?"

She chuckled softly. "I'm not really sure. I don't know what to expect."

"I'm sure it'll be fine," he said. "He's been no trouble at all while he's been here. He actually helped with a project."

Lynda was surprised. "What kind of project?" she asked.

"We were cleaning the storage area. It was a mess. He was a big help; he carried heavy boxes and mopped the floor."

"Really? That's good to hear. I'm glad he was able to be productive while he was here." Lynda always felt that how Ben behaved when he was away from her, was more important than how he behaved at home. She was pleasantly surprised that he had been helpful.

She followed Officer Hughes through the doors to the holding area. Ben was sitting on the bunk in the cell, reading a book. She tilted her head a bit, so she could see the cover and read the title. It was *To Kill a Mockingbird*. That was one of Lynda's all-time favorites. Interesting that he was reading it.

He looked up when he heard them approach.

"Hi Momma," he said. "Can I come home now?"

Lynda was fighting back tears. There was nothing more that she wanted than for him to come home.

"Yes, honey, you can," she said.

Officer Hughes unlocked the cell door and held it wide. Ben picked up the drawstring bag that Lynda had brought him the other night. As he walked out of the cell, he handed *To Kill a Mockingbird* to Officer Hughes.

"Did you finish it?" the officer asked.

"No, I'm about half-way," Ben replied.

"You keep it, then. It's one of my favorites. You should finish it."

Ben grinned. "Okay, thanks," he said. "I'll bring it back to you when I'm done."

"There will be a hearing before the judge, because of the possession charge," Officer Hughes said to Lynda as he walked them back to the lobby. "You'll both need to appear. You'll receive a letter in the mail about the date."

"Okay, I'll keep an eye out for that," she said. "Will I need to hire a lawyer?"

"Legally, I can't tell you if you'll need a lawyer or not," replied Officer Hughes. "But, in my experience, since it's his first offense, it shouldn't be too painful. He'll probably be assigned community service."

Lynda and Ben drove in silence. She had decided earlier in the day that she would not yell at him, or lecture him. That didn't seem to accomplish much.

Instead, she asked if he wanted to grab something to eat on the way home.

"Sure, what are you thinking?" Ben asked.

"I don't care, whatever you like."

"Chick-Fil-A?" Lynda knew that's what he would ask for. It was his favorite.

"Sure, let's go."

Lynda bought dinner for the two of them from the drive-through window. When they arrived home, Ben carried the bags in the house and set them on the island.

"Mom, do you want something to drink?" he asked.

"Just water, honey," Lynda replied as she pulled the stools close to the island.

They were both silent as they ate. Lynda did not want to push things with Ben. She knew he would talk when he was ready. Maybe.

Lynda had been agonizing about how to handle her son. She wanted to have complete control over him, and make absolutely sure he was not doing anything he shouldn't be. She wanted to take the handcuffs that Officer Hughes gave her, and cuff him Ben to his bed frame. That way she would know exactly where he was, every minute of the day.

But, she knew that wasn't realistic. Ben knew what his mom expected from him. She would let him know that she wasn't going to micro-manage him. But, he needed to understand that certain behavior would bring specific consequences.

If he chose to continue using drugs then he wouldn't have a smart phone, and he definitely wouldn't be getting his driver's license any time soon. On the other hand, if Ben chose to follow the simple rules of Lynda's home he could pretty much have whatever he wanted. She was lucky that she earned a decent salary, so she could afford to provide him with a smart phone. She had also planned to send him to driving school, which wasn't cheap. In Texas either the parent taught the child themselves, or the kiddo needed to attend a driving school. Lynda remembered the days when Driver's Ed was taught in public high school. Apparently it didn't work like that anymore.

The last thing Lynda wanted to do was put a stoner behind the wheel. She refused to do that. While the effect wouldn't be the same as driving while intoxicated with alcohol, there was still a certain level of impairment. The police might not be able to conduct an on-the-spot breathalyzer test for marijuana, but Lynda was certain that it couldn't be safe.

What she longed for, what she truly wanted for her son, was for him to accept responsibility for his actions. Lynda was so worried that he would go through life as the victim, blaming everyone else for his circumstances.

Everyone made mistakes in life. She had certainly made many throughout her own. But she always tried to learn from those mistakes, and to own them. And, ultimately, to not repeat those mistakes.

Lynda believed that most things that happen in a person's life are a direct reaction to the choices that person makes. People have much more control over their lives than they realize. Of course, there will be freak accidents, but no one has control over those. You can't worry constantly about what you can't control.

She could worry constantly that the company she works for might lay her off, but what good would worrying do? It's just a lot of wasted energy that could be applied to something positive, such as learning how to make homemade pasta from scratch. Besides, continuous worrying is bad for your health.

Taking responsibility for your actions and accepting the consequences of those actions is an extremely valuable life lesson. It shows maturity. Lynda realized that since her son was still a teenager, he had a long way to go regarding maturity. She hoped with all her heart that she could help Ben learn this lesson.

Ben sat on his bed, flipping through TV channels. He had to admit it; he was thrilled to be home. At first he had been furious with his mom for leaving him in jail. He knew that she could have just taken him home the day everything happened.

But after he had calmed down, Officer Hughes had spent some time with him. He had told Ben stories about his days with the Dallas PD. He had seen it all; robberies, murders, attempted murders. Officer Hughes relayed these tales to Ben in a very entertaining way. He felt as if he were watching CSI.

But there was always the subtle message that the officer

conveyed. Most of these crimes occurred because the perpetrator had been high on something. Sure, by the time they were committing crimes in order to get drug money, they had moved past pot. Some of them hadn't even started there; they had gone straight to heroin or meth. But Ben knew that Office Hughes was making the point that plenty of these hard criminals started out by smoking pot. Then they wanted to get higher, because marijuana just wasn't cutting it anymore.

Officer Hughes knew what he was talking about; Ben understood that. He also talked to him in a way that wasn't preachy or lecturing. He was just telling Ben stories about what it had been like to be a Dallas cop. That was it. It wasn't Scared Straight.

At night in the cell, while he lay on the bunk before he fell asleep, Ben would think about those stories. He would also think about his plans for his own life. He definitely planned on going to college and being a successful, productive member of society. He really hadn't thought that smoking pot would cause him to be anything other than successful, but now he wasn't so sure. He had heard of many successful people who got high to relax and wind down from their day. Because of these examples, he had never thought he would have any problems if pot became a regular part of his daily life.

But, he was just starting to think that he could possibly be mistaken about that. Apparently, there were other possible outcomes, which included the scenarios that Officer Hughes relayed to him. Since most of his friends got high, there was the added chance of the entire group moving steadily down a more destructive path.

Ben knew that if he wanted to be successful in life he

would need to surround himself with successful people. He had heard that mantra from many different people, including his mother. He thought about his friends, and which ones he could truly say were successful.

James was brilliant; there was no doubt about it. But the way he chose to live his life these days was not necessarily the best way to become a successful adult. Sure, it was fun, and Ben really liked getting high with James. James just didn't seem to care about anything else. Ben got that; there were many months where that had been the most important thing to him, also. He had been lucky that he could get decent enough grades without needing to expend too much effort. But the time he spent visiting the Rosemeade PD got him thinking.

He thought about Matt Martinez. He had always been a good friend. Matt and Ben had known each other forever. Matt was on the football team, and he was a great team player. He would do anything for a friend. Maybe Ben should start hanging out with Matt a little more, without the pot.

Ben clicked off the TV. His eyelids were getting heavy. He must have been more tired that he had realized. As he started dozing, he thought about how good it felt to be in his own bed.

Thursday Morning

Ben was sitting in his third period pre-Calculus class when his phone buzzed. Earlier, before school began for the day, he had run into Matt in the hallway. They both had some pretty good stories to share with each other. Ben about his holiday at the Grey Bar Hotel, and Matt about getting kicked off the football team. There was also some rumor about David Wright's house being TP'd by a couple of moms.

"So," Ben said to Matt, "I don't think I'm gonna hang out with James anymore."

"Yeah, I've been thinking the same thing," said Matt. "This is the weekend that he was going to make those dabs."

"I know. I need to tell him that I'm not coming over."

"Yeah, me too." Matt paused for a moment. "Maybe you and I can hang out. Stay at my place. I need to go job hunting. We could apply together, maybe work at the same place."

"Okay, that would be cool!"

Now, Ben looked at the text message that was displayed on his phone. It was from James.

"Come over by 4:00 on Saturday. That way we'll have time to get everything ready."

Ben considered how to reply to this text. Should he pretend to have other plans? Probably not. He was tired of lying. So he told the truth.

"Sorry, I won't be there. I changed my mind. I'm quitting."

Several minutes later, this message appeared:

"Fine. More for me. You're the one missing out."

That was it; Ben was finished with James.

James was annoyed with Ben, but he wasn't over the top angry. Matt had bailed on him, too. That was just a sign to James that they weren't really serious. They weren't true connoisseurs.

It was noon on Saturday, and he was beginning to gather the supplies he needed to extract the THC and make his honey oil. He had a length of PVC pipe, about twelve inches long and two inches in diameter. There was a cap for the pipe with a small hole drilled in the center of it. That hole was just the right size to insert the nozzle of a butane canister. James borrowed his mom's Magic Bullet (she never used it anyway) to grind the stems, leaves and several buds. The results would then be placed into the tube. James would cover the open end of the pipe with one coffee filter, held in place with a rubber band. It was perfect.

Ben and Matt had spent Saturday afternoon driving around town, filling out job applications. Ideally, they'd both love to work at the local skate shop, but there weren't any openings. It looked like their best bet would be working as hosts and bar backs at a sushi restaurant. Ben had no problem with this; he and his mom had been there many times and he was a big sushi fan. Matt preferred a thick, medium-rare steak to sushi. But he applied anyway. He knew that's what his parents expected.

The boys got back to Matt's house a little before five o'clock. They walked through the garage, into the kitchen, and they were welcomed by the wonderful aroma of onions and peppers frying.

"Hey, Mom, that smells pretty tasty! Fajitas tonight?" asked Matt.

"Yup, they'll be ready in about thirty minutes," replied Dottie. "You can set the table for me."

"Okay. We're going to hang out in my room for a bit, then we'll come out," said Matt.

"That's fine. Did you guys have any luck with job applications?" she asked.

"We applied at a lot of places, Mrs. Martinez," Ben told her. "Now I guess we just need to wait for a call back."

"Make sure you follow up in a couple of days for the ones you really want," she said. "That can really help. You guys come back out to help me in half an hour. You want a soda?"

The boys grabbed a couple cans of Cokes, then went to Matt's room.

Matt brought up the question that had been on his mind all day.

"So, what exactly is James doing today?" he asked.

"He's making dabs. It's extracting the THC from the pot plant," Ben replied.

"And it's stronger, and more concentrated, right?"

"Right. I think he learned how to do it from the Internet. Wanna take a look?" asked Ben.

"Sure, let's see what he's up to," replied Matt. "You

know he lives on the street behind me, right?"

"Dork, of course I know that! I was there with you last weekend," Ben laughed at his friend.

"Oh, yeah, that's right," said Matt, grinning. "Geez, maybe I was stoned."

"Yeah, yeah, I know. Okay, I found some videos here."

Ben had entered the search terms "dabs" and "THC extraction" into Google. The top five hits were YouTube videos. Ben clicked on the first one.

The boys watched the screen as the extraction process was explained in detail. The stems, leaves and buds were processed in a grinder. The resulting mixture was placed in a PVC tube. One end was covered with a coffee filter, secured with a rubber band. The other end was covered with a PVC cap that had a small hole in the center. Through that hole, the nozzle of a butane canister was placed. The entire can of butane was forced through the PVC tube, as the tube was held over a Pyrex dish. As the butane was forced through the marijuana, a yellow substance was strained through the coffee filter. This was the THC extraction.

Ben and Matt scrolled through the titles of several more videos.

"Hey, what's this one about?" asked Matt. He was pointing to a video that showed the title "Epic Honey Oil Fail." Apparently, the extracted THC was known by many names including honey oil, butter, shatter, and 710.

When Matt clicked on the first video, it showed the PVC pipe stuffed with the ground-up stems and leaves, and the butane canister performing the extraction into a Pyrex dish. The dish was sitting on a carpeted floor. From the end of the pipe that was covered with the coffee filter, the yellow liquid streamed out, and collected in the pan.

In the background the boys could see a pair of sneakered feet shuffling along the carpet, behind the chemist. Suddenly there was a loud "POP!" that caused Matt and Ben to jump in their chairs.

Through the computer speakers came the sounds of screaming and voices shouting, "The house is on fire! The house is on fire!"

Then the screen went black.

Matt asked, "What was that about? Why did that happen?"

"I don't know," replied Ben. "Let's see what other kinds of videos are out there."

Matt returned to the YouTube search results page.

"Click on that one," said Ben, pointing to a video entitled, "Honey oil lab causes explosion." The video was a clip from a news story in Colorado.

The petite, perfectly made-up anchorwoman came on the screen. "Last night, a house in Highlands Ranch exploded due to home-chemists extracting THC from marijuana stems, leaves and buds. The resulting product is often called 'honey oil' and offers the user a faster, more potent high than smoking marijuana alone. Todd, what's the scene like?"

The camera switched to the on-the-scene reporter. In the background, a flaming house lit up the night sky.

"Pamela, the house is in shambles. It looks like the explosion happened in the kitchen and fire quickly spread throughout the rest of the house. It's gone. Firefighters arrived on the scene within minutes, followed closely by ambulances. Two individuals have already been transported to Sky Ridge Hospital. They appeared to have been burned very badly. Back to you."

The video showed the anchorwoman again.

"Todd, how do the explosions occur?"

"They use butane to extract the THC. Butane is a heavy gas that falls instead of rises. It's also very flammable. If this task is performed around any kind of flame, like a pilot light, or even in a carpeted area where static electricity could easily develop, it can easily cause a deadly explosion."

"Thank you, Todd. Explosions due to honey oil extraction have risen during the past year. In the Denver Metro area we've seen a total of fourteen since January."

That was the end of the video. The boys were silent.

"Do you want to watch another one?" Matt asked.

"No," replied Ben. "I think that's enough." He paused. "Do you think James knows what he's doing? He's really smart. He knows how to be safe with this, right?"

At that moment, both boys jumped in their chairs. *Pop! Pop! Pop!* It sounded like Fourth of July fireworks were going off right in the backyard.

"What the hell was that?" yelled Ben, as he rushed to the window. Matt's bedroom faced the backyard, and was on the second story of the house. From this vantage point, Ben had a good view of the block of houses behind them.

Ben easily identified James' house which was on the street directly behind Matt's, and about five houses to the right. The sun was just starting to set behind Ben, causing his view to be shrouded in shadows. But he didn't need any sunlight to see; the dimness caused by approaching twilight made it easier to see the flames that were on the first floor of James' house. Ben could see the orange and yellow light dancing through the kitchen window.

"Holy shit! Call 911!" he yelled.

Matt grabbed his phone and dialed, as he also stared at the blaze that was growing larger every second.

"We have to get over there," said Ben.

He thundered down the stairs, taking them two at a time. Matt was right behind him, talking to the 911 dispatcher.

Dottie came out of the kitchen, wondering why it sounded like a herd of elephants was running through her house.

"James' house is on fire!" Matt called to her over his shoulder. "I called the fire department. We need to go make sure he's okay!"

Before she could object, the boys were out the door.

In Matt's neighborhood most of the streets were separated by alleys. Garages were behind the houses, instead of in front. Kids often cut between houses in order to avoid biking or running all the way around the various streets. These shortcuts made it easy for Ben and Matt to quickly sprint to James' house.

They ran into Matt's garage. Ben punched the electronic opener, and both boys danced in frustration, waiting for the door to roll up. Before it had reached the half-way point, they crouched low and shuffled underneath it, running into the driveway and the alley beyond.

Ben reached James' house first; the firetrucks weren't even there yet, but he could hear the sirens in the distance. Matt reached his friend's side a second later. Now that they were there, they weren't sure what to do. They knew they needed to help their friend, but they were both very wary about entering a burning building.

Ben cautiously walked across the front lawn toward the

house. He peered through the living room window. He could see the fire, but it didn't appear to be at the front of the house. It seemed contained, toward the back.

He walked to the front door and placed his hand on it. It was not hot. He tried the knob; it turned easily in his hand. Ever so gingerly, he slowly opened the door, ready to spring back if the fire threatened.

"James!" he called loudly. "James, are you in there?"

The smoke was already thick, and getting worse every second. Ben took one step inside.

"James!" he called again.

Through the curtain of smoke, he heard a cough.

"James, where are you?"

The cough came again.

Ben got on his belly and army-crawled toward that sound. He could barely see anything, but he kept going. He bumped his head on the leg of a chair and realized he must be in the dining room. The smoke was getting thicker.

He maneuvered around the chair and crawled forward. His head struck another object, but this didn't feel like furniture. Ben reached forward with his hand, and felt hair on someone's head. It was James! But he wasn't moving.

Ben yanked hard on James' hair. The coughing started again.

"Come on James!" Ben screamed in his face. "We have to go!"

He grabbed James by the arm and started dragging him toward the front door. Geez, he was heavy; Ben was dragging dead weight.

He gave James' hair a good, hard pull in an effort to get him moving. James sputtered, and seemed to regain some consciousness. Still gripping James' arm, Ben crawled toward the exit once again. James was actually helping a little, which helped them move much more quickly.

The door should have been wide open, but Ben was having a very hard time seeing it through the smoke. He thought they were getting close. Suddenly, he heard Matt calling his name.

"Ben! Come this way!"

Ben and James crawled toward the sound. Ben was still mostly dragging James, but at least he was conscious.

Suddenly, Ben felt big, rough hands grab him by the shoulders and practically hurl him through the open door. He gulped fresh air into his lungs. He hadn't known it could feel so good to breathe the clean air.

He was taken to an ambulance, and examined by an EMT. The paramedic was checking his heart rate, blood pressure, and his lung function. Ben was beginning to feel much better.

"Everything sounds pretty good," the EMT said. "Your lungs sound fine, so I don't think you were in there long enough to do any damage. Do you think you need to go to the hospital?"

"No, I think I'm okay," replied Ben. "How's James?"

"I think he's pretty badly burned. They're getting him ready to transport him to Presbyterian Hospital right now."

Ben looked toward the other ambulance. He couldn't see much; there was a lot of chaos happening all around him. Firefighters were still working on putting out the fire inside the house. He could see Matt and Dottie standing with a group of onlookers; the commotion had obviously piqued the interest of the neighbors, who wanted to see what was happening.

"Ben!" he heard his name being called from somewhere in the crowd.

"Mom?" he answered.

"Ben!" she called again. Then he saw her break through the crowd, and run to the ambulance where he was being examined. She threw her arms around him before performing her own examination. Lynda needed to make sure he didn't have any broken or missing parts.

"Oh my god, Ben, what happened?" she asked.

Ben gave her the consolidated version of everything that happened that evening. He explained how he and Matt had become worried when they watched the YouTube videos on how to extract THC and create dabs. Then, when they heard what sounded like fireworks and saw the fire from Matt's room, Ben was led by instinct and did what he could to save his friend.

"Running into a burning house is pretty damn stupid," said the EMT. He had been listening to the whole story. "But I'll say this; I don't think your friend would be alive if you hadn't gotten him out when you did."

Lynda and Ben watched the ambulance slowly start moving, to take James to the hospital. Lynda kept her arm around her son's shoulders. She knew how lucky she was; how lucky they both were. It could very easily been Ben who was being transported to the hospital to be treated for who knew what kinds of burns. But it wasn't. She had never felt as grateful as she did at that moment.

Epilogue

Ben rang up the popcorn sale and told the customer, "That'll be $22.46, please." He swiped the debit card, and told the couple to enjoy their movie.

The theater was busier than he thought it would be on Christmas Day. But then again, he supposed a lot of people went to the movies after enjoying a big Christmas dinner. He had been hired by Cinemark shortly after the explosion. Matt was working at Cabela's so they weren't able to spend time together on the job. But that was okay. Between school and work they were both pretty busy, and they hung out together when there was time.

Ben was pouring popcorn kernels into the popper when he noticed three customers approaching the concession counter. At first he thought they were just another typical family; mom, dad, and teenage son. But as they approached, he noticed that something didn't look quite right with the son. He walked with a pronounced limp. His face was terribly scarred. There was a patch over his right eye. Then Ben recognized him. It was James.

Ben had visited James once while he was in the hospital. He knew that James' total stay had been about three weeks. Ben had stopped by about one week into that time. It was not a fun visit. James' face and hands had been severely burned by the fire. A shard of glass from a baking dish that had been blown to smithereens had lodged itself deeply in his right thigh. He had been in terrible pain and wasn't in the mood for visitors.

Ben had really just wanted to see him and make sure he would survive. On the night he had dragged James from the burning house, Ben had had no idea how badly James was hurt. And now, as the trio walked toward the counter, he looked very different than the friend Ben used to know.

James placed his hands on the glass counter top and said, "Hi Ben." He sounded happy, and was actually smiling a bit crookedly. "It's great to see you! Hey, I want you to meet my parents."

James' mother stepped forward with a large grin on her face. She grasped Ben's hand in both of hers.

"Hello, Ben. I'm so happy to meet you. We are so grateful to you. James wouldn't be here today if it weren't for you," she said. Her eyes were shining with unshed tears.

"It's nice to meet you." Ben was feeling self-conscious beneath all of this praise. "I just did what anyone would have done."

James' dad chuckled. "I don't really think that's true," he said. "Thank you, Ben. If there's anything we can ever do for you, I want you to ask. Really."

"We're going to see the new Chris Pratt movie," said James.

"Oh, yeah, it's really good. I've seen it three times already. Enjoy the show."

"I'll see you around school," replied James. "Bye, Ben."

"Yeah, I'll see you. Good-bye."

James' dad placed his hand on his son's shoulder as Ben

watched them walk away. They handed their tickets to the usher and walked into the darkness of the theater. But Ben thought they were really walking into the light of a new beginning.

SMOKE SCREEN

Book Club Discussion Questions

1. How do you feel about the legalization of marijuana for both medicinal and recreational purposes?
2. Even in the states that have legalized marijuana, if you don't want it to be used in your home do you think those rules should be followed?
3. How much power should a teenager have in the home?
4. Should a single mother be less or more strict with her children?
5. Did Lynda do the right thing when she called the parents of other teenagers who were smoking pot? Or, was that none of her business?

Other Work by Diane Windsor
All of Diane's books can be found at:
www.MotinaBooks.com
How To Relationship – A Relationship Guide for Teens
with Divorced Parents
How to CoParent During the Holidays
Calming, Art Therapy Coloring Book for Single Moms

If you are a teacher or other education professional,
contact us to receive a free teacher's guide for *Smoke Screen*.